OUR SHARED HUMANITY

Finding Common Ground in a Divisive World

Gudjon Bergmann

Table of Contents

Dedication

To our shared humanity

Foreword: Division Lead Me to This Work

In 2017, I went on one of my contemplative walks. On this particular fall day, division was on my mind. I was reflecting on the outrage and anger that seemed so pervasive on social media; the street violence that I had witnessed with increasing frequency in the news; the friendships and romantic relationships I had seen splinter because of differing ideologies; the strained family gatherings I had attended in recent years; the feelings of dread and fear that had been conveyed to me by Muslim friends in the interfaith community; the race-related rhetoric that was getting more toxic and contentious every day; and the anti-religious sentiment that was growing louder among many of my non-religious friends.

All of this was affecting me, creating feelings of irritation, anger, and frustration. 'What if this continues,' I thought to myself. 'What if the forces of division become stronger and stronger every year? Where will it end in five, ten, or fifteen years?' I allowed my imagination to carry me into the future as I considered the answers. What I saw in my mind's eye wasn't pretty. 'Something has to be done!' That was my thinking when I returned from my walk.

Thankfully, I stumbled on the following quote from Nobel Peace Prize laureate Betty Williams:

"Turmoil is everywhere, and the whole world is waiting for solutions to come from the top down. That's now how it works—community change from the bottom up makes a real difference."

"From the bottom up!"

Those words caught my attention. Waiting for the federal government, my state government, local city council, or even well-meaning organizations to solve any of this wasn't likely to bear fruit... but I could work from the bottom up. I could use my talents for teaching and writing to have an impact.

I could throw my stone in the pond and hope it would create ripples.

I could do something.

So I did. I played to my strengths and started by gathering ideas and practical strategies from a variety of sources—including peacemakers and Nobel laureates—developed talks that turned into an official initiative, created an online program that I offered in partnership with Charter for Compassion, and wrote a book titled Co-Human Harmony that focused on improved relations between people of faith. In 2020, the Charter asked me to do a version of that program with less of an emphasis on faith. That is when Our Shared Humanity was born.

Of course, I haven't changed the world with any of my efforts. That was never the goal. Yet, I have reached thousands of people since I started this work and that has created ripples. What little I have done is already being felt farther away than I could have anticipated. On the following pages, I hope to encourage you to do what you can, with what you have, where you are. That is all I have done and will continue to do.

Gudjon Bergmann
Author and Interfaith Minister
www.gudjonbergmann.com

Email: bergmann@gudjonbergmann.com
Facebook: www.facebook.com/bergmanngudjon
Twitter: @gudjonbergmann

1. Overcoming the Normalization of Division

Why do people seek peace and harmony? The answer to that question is simple. People seek harmony when they experience acrimony and discord. When life is good there is no need to seek something better. It's only when the rhythm of life is disrupted that people pay attention.

The obvious follow-up question is 'how much discomfort are we talking about here?' It differs. Some people have trained themselves to live in a continual state of harmony and the slightest disturbance will prompt them to recalibrate. Others have, knowingly or unknowingly, numbed or hardened themselves to the forces of discord so that nothing short of a catastrophe will get their attention.

In recent years, we have witnessed the normalization of division. Tensions have risen to a crescendo and we are all feeling the pain. Thankfully, this also means that more and more people are willing to do something about it.

Extremism Leads to Division

The central problem leading to all this division appears to be extremism. In the simplest terms, extremism is based on a belief that one group is right and everyone else is wrong. When people believe that they are right, any measure is justified while defending, propagating, and advancing 'the truth' as they see it. Whether the doctrine is political or theological, extremism thrives on absolutist terms. There is no room for other views. In fact, those who harbor other views are labeled as the enemy, making it easier to vilify and dehumanize.

How Extremism is Perpetuated

Two factors are needed for the creation and perpetuation of extremism.

First, a close-knit group with shared beliefs. In the old days, people were constrained by geography, which made it harder to form extremist groups. In the digital age, finding like-minded people is easier than ever, which partly explains the modern rise of extremism.

Second, propaganda. Psychology tells us that to influence the human mind, a mix of (i) personal identification, (ii) repetition, and (iii) strong emotion are needed.

When people find themselves identifying with a certain group due to their ideology ("I believe that too"), and are constantly (repetition) seeing memes/posts that enrage (strong emotion), they are being radicalized. Sharing those ideas then perpetuates the cycle of propaganda and leads to even more extremism.

If you think about it, this is a first for humanity. Before social media, we needed to congregate in person to get the same results. Now, all we need to do is go on our devices and the exposure is relentless.

Breaking the Cycle

What can we do?

Well, understanding the psychology is an important first step. Constant repetition combined with strong emotions will, intentionally or not, change neural pathways. Constant neurological exposure is like driving on a dirt road and strong emotions are like rain. The wetter the terrain, the deeper the tracks get with every repetition.

Seeing the consequences comes next. Clarity will come quickly to those who are willing to take a step back and look objectively at what is going on. Once we acknowledge cause and effect, that will lead to the third step; breaking the cycle. We can stop participating in polarizing behavior and choose a better path.

Choosing a Better Narrative

Let's back up a moment and ask a few questions that must be on your mind, just like they were on mine when I started to look for common ground, questions like: Are peace and harmony even possible? Can they ever be achieved on a communal level? Isn't man condemned to live in a state of constant strife and struggle? Is there any example in history of social harmony on a large scale?

These are all are reasonable questions. In an attempt to answer them, allow me to quote someone much wiser than myself. Gandhi wrote the following passage in his book, Non-Violent Resistance (Satyagraha), and it offers us the possibility of a new narrative.

"History, as we know it, is a record of the wars of the world, and so there is a proverb among Englishmen that a nation which has no history, that is, no wars, is a happy nation. How kings played, how they became the enemies of one another, how they murdered one another, is found accurately recorded in history, and if this were all that had happened in the world, it would have ended long ago. If the story of the universe had commenced with wars, not a man would have been found alive today [...] The fact that there are so many men still alive in the world shows that it is based not on the force of arms but on the force of truth or love. Therefore, the greatest and most unimpeachable evidence of the success of this force is to be found in the fact that, in spite of the wars of the world, it still lives on. [...] Little quarrels of millions of families in their daily lives disappear before the exercise of this force. Hundreds of nations live in peace. History

does not and cannot take note of this fact. History is really a record of every interruption of the even working of the force of love or of the soul. Two brothers quarrel; one of them repents and re-awakens the love that was lying dormant in him; the two again begin to live in peace; nobody takes note of this. But if the two brothers, through the intervention of solicitors or some other reason, take up arms or go to law—which is another form of the exhibition of brute force—their doing would be immediately noticed in the press, they would be the talk of their neighbors and would probably go down in history. And what is true of families and communities is true of nations. There is no reason to believe that there is one law for families and another for nations. History, then, is a record of an interruption of the course of nature. Soul-force, being natural, is not noted in history."

Gandhi makes a strong argument in this passage. Soul-force is the rule, not the exception. Modern news coverage reflects his theory. Only disruptive events are reported while a vast majority of people go about their daily lives in peace and are not deemed newsworthy.

Based on this reasoning, we need to stop seeing people as naturally divisive. Our new narrative can be that compassion and harmony are natural forces that most people choose when given the chance. For that new way of thinking to stick, we need to continually remind ourselves that the so-called soul-force has been sustained in some form in every society throughout the ages. We would not be here today if it were the other way around.

The Democratic Dilemma

Democracies all around the globe are engaged in a grand experiment of self-governance. The balance is tricky. For the democratic process to work, all citizens must be committed to the peaceful transfer of power and to solving problems through dialogue and lawful behavior rather than coercion and violence. On one end, people are committed to living harmoniously and in peace; on the other, they have vigorous debates about how to best run the government that they have chosen to serve them.

As mentioned earlier, compromise is a key element in this context. If a group of citizens decides, "it's our way or the highway," then the results are discontent and turmoil. Such unrest can lead to violent surges and that opens the door for rule through brute force. Historically, we've seen examples of this in dictatorships and during the rise of fascist governments, where social unrest has led the government to conclude that the people are no longer 'trusted' to rule themselves. Benjamin Franklin aptly wrote that:

"Only a virtuous people are capable of freedom. As nations become corrupt and vicious, they have more need of masters."

The constant otherizing and dehumanizing of the past few years has sown seeds, fertilizing the ground for the possibility of physical violence or disenfranchisement of segments of the population. If we want to avoid the worst possible outcomes and stop acrimony from further spilling into the streets, we need active groups of peacemakers, bridge-builders, and harmonizers in every community. We must heed the words of Dr. Martin Luther King Jr. who said:

"Those who love peace must learn to organize as effectively as those who love war."

An Achievable Vision for the Future

The question we are faced with is a difficult one. How can we move this idea of soul-force, peace, and harmony from the theoretical realm and into our daily lives? From a realistic standpoint, we have to admit that human beings will never be in complete harmony with each other. Singing Kumbaya by the campfire is reserved for smaller groups, not the whole of humanity. There are just too many disparate views and competing interests for that to happen... but we can do better.

With that in mind, I've come up with what I believe to be an achievable vision for the future. Here's my thinking. According to sociologists, the average human being has the ability to truly connect with somewhere between 40-120 people. Within this core group are friends, co-workers, family members and others that the person feels he or she can trust. We are not talking about the thousands of social media connections that some people have, rather the people that they turn to in times of need. Now, imagine one or two willing and able people in every group who serve as mediators and peacemakers, who seek common ground rather than conflict, and who are comfortable with being around others that don't believe or look as they do. Those one or two people can work openly towards finding common ground from within the group and connect them with other groups.

One or two people per group.

That's all it takes to influence group dynamics.

And that creates ripples.

An Illustrative Musical Analogy

A participant in one of my workshops presented the perfect musical analogy to illustrate my vision. She regularly joins a group of people who play Irish folk songs, and they seldom use sheet music. Because everyone is welcome to join this ensemble, participants learn the tunes on their own or pick them up from each other. It's usually pretty chaotic. However, the insertion of one or two outstanding musicians can have two effects. If the musicians try to show off, then the whole group suffers and people either withdraw or struggle to keep up. If, on the other hand, the musicians are patient and supportive of the group, then everyone plays better. One or two qualified people can have a ripple effect that is measurable on everything from rhythm to tone.

One or two people.

Supportive. Patient.

Those are the keywords to remember.

Making Peace a Priority

As I mentioned earlier, our need for harmony is in direct relationship with the amount of acrimony we feel. Several years ago, I spoke with a minister who was teaching in the outskirts of New York on 9/11 2001. He told me that he'd never seen strangers come together as they did in the weeks after the attack on the Twin Towers. People went out of their way to be nice to each other, support each other, smile, and lend a helping hand. He has not experienced anything like it since. In fact, he jokingly mentioned that an alien invasion might be the only way to bring humanity together in a similar fashion.

The truth is that work towards finding common ground and living in harmony often dissipates with receding acrimony. People start to feel better and get sidetracked. This is natural. However, those of us who want to build bridges and find common ground have to work against this instinctive tendency. We have to make the work important, either by continually re-

minding ourselves of the worst that can happen or en-
visioning the kind of world that we want to live in and
work towards that every day. Some days the carrot will
be enough to spur us to action. Other days only a
vivid mental image of the stick will do the trick.

What About Social Justice?

In recent years, several participants in my workshops
have told me that they are not interested in social
harmony or finding common ground; they want social
justice. I understand that. However, while the two approaches are different, they are not polar opposites. In
fact, they can complement each other.

The social harmony approach looks for potential
bridge-building opportunities and attempts to find
common ground before trying to solve difficult issues.

The social justice approach seeks to highlight injus-
tices in the public domain, draw attention to them in
any way it can, and then solve them through legal re-
forms. In many cases, anger and outrage are used as
catalysts.

The two can work together. If people want society to
be just, it must also be peaceful (which was the reason
why Rev. Martin Luther King Jr. was so focused on
nonviolence). Once an injustice has been uncovered in
the public arena and the fight has taken place for long
enough, then the forces of social harmony can come

in with bridge-building techniques to establish relations for the future. Sooner or later people have to sit
down and talk to find compromise. That is easier to do
when bridges between different groups exist. Con-
versely, if all the bridges have been burnt and people
are shouting at each other in righteous rage from opposite ends of ideological chasms then no minds will
be changed and no peace will be found.

We need communications and dialogue based on
trust. We need to see how we are alike. We need to
hold onto the idea that finding common ground is not
only possible but that it is based on the very soul-force
that holds communities and families together.

We Can Be the Change

If you are ready to start working on this simple vision
of finding common ground and strengthening the
soul-force in yourself and your community, join me in
a simple pledge of responsibility:

Even if we did not create the acrimony, even if we
weren't the ones who created the divide, we can be
bridge-builders, healers, harmonizers, and a vital part
of the solution. We can reach out across divides that
we did not create for the sake of finding common
ground. We can cause positive reverberations to offset
negative discord. We can be the change we want to see
in the world.

PERSONAL INITIATIVES

Status Check

Answering the following questions in writing will clarify your current position. In the same way that you need to know your location before you plot a new course on a map, it can be helpful to know where you stand in relation to peace and harmony before you attempt to make improvements.

1. What kind of divisions do you see in our society that you want to bridge?
2. What triggers you about other people's behavior?
3. Do you spend any time with people who have different ideologies than you do (religious, spiritual, political, nutritional, success, etc.)? If yes, how do those interactions usually go (i.e., where do they land on the spectrum of harmony)?
4. What are the biggest external obstacles you see before common ground can be found within your society?
5. What are the biggest internal obstacles you see before common ground can be found within your society?

Two Lists for Reflection

The following two lists demonstrate the most common reasons why people have come to my lectures and workshops. One list reveals an aversion to acrimony where pain and displeasure are the driving forces behind people's decisions to attend. The other list describes constructive intentions where attendees want to do something to counter the forces of division and are looking for solutions. I urge you to take a moment and read through them. Reflect on your motives for reading this book while you explore other people's aversions and aspirations.

Aversion to Acrimony:

- "I am painfully aware of the cost of disharmony in my personal life, my relationships, and in the world."
- "I stopped interacting with people due to differences in religious ideology."
- "I visited Jerusalem and was dismayed by the enmity between Jewish and Muslim residents there."
- "There is such a divide in the US politically right now. My friends and family appear to want the same things, peace and happiness, yet they have totally different political beliefs. I find myself unable to communicate with them."
- "I am disheartened by the lack of civility and dehumanizing rhetoric these days."
- "Friends, who I've known for twenty years, are suddenly strangers whom I can't talk to... our differences a gulf between us."
- "These are dark times. There are so many areas of conflict between countries, religions, genders, cultures, generations, and political ideologies."

- "I am always looking for the final strike, the last shoe to drop. I am tired of crying."
- "I am a Christian minister and the divisive rhetoric within the 'camps' of Christianity belies the message we are to promote. I need to do a better job of affirming my beliefs without dismissing, demeaning or discounting others."
- "I am exhausted."
- "As a social worker, I tried to be compassionate and understanding. Now that I have retired, I sometimes allow myself the easy way out and just look at what is wrong with the other person's point of view."
- "I have concerns about the rising levels of rancor in public discourse and my own increasing anxiety about it all."

Seeking Solutions:

- "I am engaged in a mission to reduce poverty, organize educational opportunities, and create positive practices. I am intrigued by this approach."
- "I want to uncover strategies to celebrate differences both in my academic work and in my life."
- "I am looking for tools for building harmonious relationships within diverse communities."
- "I have an active interest in interfaith dialogue and harmony."
- "I want to gain skills to communicate effectively and compassionately."

- "I will be a better citizen and teacher if I learn strategies for building bridges."
- "I want to learn practical ways to communicate with people that I disagree with without compromising my values or losing myself."
- "I want to be reminded of the fact that people are fundamentally kind."
- "I am participating to be more comfortable with asking good questions, to increase my listening skills, and be more able to respond with compassion—a little at a time."
- "I am nudging myself back to a more compassionate perspective."
- "I am a professor of politics and am looking for ideas to add to my curriculum."
- "I have decided to initiate a bridge-building program in my apartment building and am looking for tools."
- "I want to generate fertile ground for my granddaughter and future generations."

2. Finding Common Ground

Padraig O'Malley, who was instrumental in the Northern Ireland peace process, said that we all have two personas, the human and the ideological. His observation was that in order to dehumanize someone, we need to start seeing him or her as an ideologue only. That diminishes our shared humanity and creates a vacuum for violence. Ever since I came across his simple idea, it has been at the heart of my efforts to find common ground.

The Ideological Persona

The ideological persona consists of beliefs and values—including ideas, stories, and principles—that people have chosen—through reason, emotion or repetition—to put faith in, even though there is little empirical evidence to either prove or disprove their validity. The distinguishing feature is belief. Most ideologies cannot be independently proven or disproven, which is why arguments can be made for or against almost any conceptual stance and people can be swayed by ideological rhetoric.

The ideological persona plays an important role in our lives. It develops with more consistency during adolescence as our likes and dislikes become clearer and matures into a central part of our character as we age. Beliefs and values provide us with a moral compass, an identity, connections to groups of like-minded people, and a sense of purpose, to name a few.

Once it has matured, the ideological persona makes up our personal philosophy and produces the color of the glasses through which we view and interpret life. It incorporates all types of ideologies, including: politics (how we believe society should be run), religion and spirituality (what we believe to be of utmost importance), morality (how we believe we should behave and treat each other), success (what it means to be successful), nutrition (what we should eat—which is currently a blend of evidence and ideology)... and much more

Once ideologies have been developed, categorized, and are consistently utilized they become –isms, such as capitalism, creationism, egalitarianism, environmentalism, existentialism, fascism, feminism, fundamentalism, humanism, imperialism, impressionism, isolationism, legalism, militarism, pacifism, pantheism, polytheism, racism, realism, romanticism, scholasticism, skepticism, socialism, surrealism, totalitarianism, utilitarianism ...et cetera, et cetera... (there is no shortage of –isms).

In this context, it would be nice if people would preface their belief and value statements with sentences like: "I believe..." "What I think..." "I value..." "I prefer..." "My view is..." ...and so on, but ideologies often become so ingrained that they fuse with empirical facts and people stop seeing them for what they are, namely, beliefs and values. Instead, people present their ideologies as factual statements. Getting them to acknowledge that their beliefs and values are, in fact, beliefs and values is often an important step in the direction of lessening tensions and finding common ground.

It goes without saying that not everyone shares the same ideologies, beliefs, or values, especially in a diverse society, which means that the ideological persona provides us with both opportunities and obstacles.

Ideological persona = Beliefs and values that cannot be independently proven or disproven

The Human Persona

The human persona consists of elements that are shared by every other human being on the planet. Maslow's hierarchy of needs is a good place to start when we are trying to understand our shared humanity. The model is usually presented in a pyramid for-

mat, with basic needs at the bottom and self-actualization needs at the top.

Similarities abound when we look at the basics. Every
human being has physiological needs for food, shelter,
water, warmth, and rest, and has safety needs, including requirements for security, a steady job or income,
and more. Most of us fulfill these rudimentary needs
in similar ways.

Our paths diverge somewhat when it comes to belong-
ingness needs—including intimate relationships,
friendships, and esteem needs—since the variety of
ways in which they can be satisfied is greater.

Still, because the first four needs are so-called defi-
ciency needs—meaning that human beings usually
pursue them until they are met—most everyone res-
onates with other human beings and understands why
they are doing what they are doing when they are attempting to satisfy the four basic needs. However,
when it comes to self-actualization needs, people are
vastly different in their approaches and ideologies
(ideological persona) and less similarity can be found
by comparing them.

This means that the lower the needs are in the pyramid and the more fundamental they are to our existence, the easier it is to connect through them. In fact,
making a connection with another human persona
can often feel instinctual at the basic level because we

share more elements with less diversity. Let me give you a few examples:

Hosting: A generous host can easily connect with the human persona in his guests by (1) offering food, water, warmth, and rest, (2) attending to safety and security, (3) offering friendship, and (4) making them feel worthwhile.

Natural disasters: Human-to-human connections are frequently on full display during natural disasters. People set aside ideological differences and do their best to help fellow human beings that they do not know. There are no screener questions to check for ideological purity, only a shared sense of compassion because everyone's needs at that moment are the same.

Children: Many people find it easy to relate to children, especially babies because they have not yet developed a robust ideological identity (incidentally, the same can be said about pets since they share basic survival needs and some emotional components but have no well-defined ideological persona).

Celebrities (opposite): As an example of the opposite, people are often disappointed when athletes and actors—with whom they have shared strong empathy—express ideological views that are different from their own because the sense of shared humanity feels somehow diminished

Obviously, making human-to-human connections becomes more difficult as complexity increases. Once we get to emotional needs, for example, a wide range of human emotions can make it challenging for people to relate to each other.

Interestingly enough, the lowest common emotional denominator is not happiness (even though offering a smile rarely fails), but rather suffering. Everyone feels miserable at one point or another in his or her life, which means that pain can serve as a mega-connector for human beings in the right circumstances. Evidence of friendships and support groups around the world clearly shows this. If I am vulnerable enough to share my pain with you and you have experienced something similar (or can imagine my pain), then we have made an instant human connection. The poet, Henry Wadsworth Longfellow, rightly observed that:

"If we could read the secret history of our enemies, we should find in each man's life sorrow and suffering enough to disarm all hostility."

Studying Maslow's human needs can give insights into the essential elements that constitute the human persona, but that's only the beginning. I encourage you to strengthen your understanding of our shared humanity with both personal observations and the exploration of other psycho-spiritual, sociological, behavioral, and anthropological models.

To see the human persona clearly, look for things that we all share, regardless of ideological differences.

Human persona = Universally shared human elements

Two Extremes

As far as I can tell, there are two extremes related to this idea of the two personas. One extreme is the danger of dehumanization. When people focus on ideological differences and consistently refer to each other using discriminating labels, then a door has been opened to alienating 'the other' and making the human being somehow less than human. That creates justifications to deny basic human needs, a willingness to go along with social marginalization, and a readiness to condone violence. Once violence is condoned, the otherizing is complete.

The other extreme claims that "we are all the same" and misinterprets any attempt to discuss differing beliefs as an attack on someone's humanity. Ideological differences are dismissed as trivial and only the human persona is allowed to exist. The mere mention of differences is seen as an attack. This kind of reductionism can also cause problems, but they are different in kind, since people who refuse to see ideological differences usually do not resort to violence.

The Most Important Project

From an integral standpoint, every human being is a complex mix of these two personas, but our information-driven society has placed an overemphasis on the ideological persona. That has created an imbalance, politicizing and polarizing everything in ideological terms; from word-use to basic human characteristics such as gender and skin color. Based on this discrepancy, I can say without hesitation that the most important project at this moment in history is to reclaim a social connection to the human persona, to move away from dehumanizing and otherizing in the direction of co-humanizing. Before we delve into solutions, let's take a closer look at the problem through the prism of the two personas.

Extreme Ideological Labeling

"These people. What these people don't understand is…" That's how it often starts. Otherizing begins innocently enough, but before we know it, we're stuck on a slippery slope to extremism. Attempts to create a little bit of an ideological distance often end in full-blown labeling where no shared humanity is allowed. As such, most labeling starts out generically. In the political realm, it begins with something mundane like liberal or conservative, but can then devolve quickly into something much nastier like baby-killer and gun-nut.

Obviously, labeling is not restricted to politics and the escalation can be intense. As divides grow, Muslims become towel-heads and terrorists, Christians become gay-haters and hypocrites, poor people become losers and takers, believers become religious-nuts and zealots, atheists become the spawns of Satan... and on it goes. The more extreme the labels become, the easier it is to stop seeing 'the other' as fully human.

With such overuse of ideological rhetoric, people create aliens in their own backyards. How can people love their neighbor as themselves if they cannot see their own humanity reflected in their neighbor?

Lack of Nuance

The social sciences have shown that people's beliefs are more nuanced than they appear to be. Believers in a particular cause or ideology may have core values in common with their group, but, when they get a chance to illustrate their personal preferences in detail, most of them employ a sliding scale with some variations. Knowing that should serve as a welcome relief. People are not homogenous; their beliefs are more varied than they appear to be.

Unfortunately, this reality can be easily overlooked from a distance. From the opposite side of a socially created chasm, the view is often black and white with no room for shades of gray. Anyone who slightly associates with a specific worldview is perceived as believing the most extreme versions of that ideology.

Such an inaccurate perception creates cognitive dissonance. What is true about us—in essence, that our beliefs and values exist in shades of gray, that we are not extremists—can not be true about the other side, or, at least, that is what we think.

The problem is that without having direct conversations, we cannot ascertain for ourselves whether beliefs are nuanced or if people are as fanatical as we imagine them to be. For the sake of social harmony, we need to be willing to explore the possibility of finding nuance for three reasons; (1) nuanced beliefs are the de facto human mindset, (2) if people are treated like extremists, they can rise to the occasion, and (3) people, who are not extremists, can start to see others who employ extremist labels indiscriminately as extremists themselves, leaving no room for bridge-building or compromise

This last point is probably the most important one. For instance, if Claire is not an extremist, but is frequently called one despite her nuanced beliefs, she will start to see those who use unjust labels about her as extremists themselves and will not want to engage with them in any way, thusly widening an already growing divide.

Social Media and the Ideological Persona

As I have already alluded to, the gap widening faster on social media than anywhere else. There is a simple reason for that. Think about it. Of the two personas, which one do you interact more with on social media?

Exactly—it's the ideological persona.

In fact, nowhere is the ideological persona more noticeable and less nuanced than on social media. Everything is black and white. You are either for or against. Shared memes and bite-size snippets work like dynamite to enlarge divides between people. Constant ideological sharing is creating more and more personal distance—even between people who've known and liked each other for a long time. "How can such and such believe that?" is one of the main complaints that I hear in my workshops.

Recognizing Our Shared Humanity in Others

To re-establish a balance between the two personas, we must find as many ways as possible to incorporate the human persona into our lives by increasing human-to-human contact and by supplementing every statement about ideological differences with a sense of shared humanity. In the words of Archbishop Desmond Tutu:

"All of our humanity is dependent upon recognizing the humanity in others."

Common ground is easier to find if we recognize that shared humanity is the underlying link that ties all of us together.

Do We All Want the Same Things?

Several years ago, I witnessed an argument on television that centered on the Middle East—a contentious topic to say the least. The interviewee had spent several years in Afghanistan, Pakistan, and Lebanon. She was giving her insights into daily life there when the interviewer asked: "What was the one thing that you took away from your experience?"

She replied: "That we all want the same things."

To which he replied: "No, we don't. No… we don't!!!"

The interviewer then angrily recounted all the ways in which the liberal West and the Middle East are different, how our values and beliefs collide, and so on.

She tried to get a word in edgewise to explain what she meant, in essence, that we all want the same things for our children, that we all want safety, security, shelter, access to sustenance, and emotional connections, but he wouldn't listen. The interview, which had been amicable up until that point, never recovered.

In the context of this chapter about the two personas, we can easily see where the quarrel originated. She was talking about the human persona while he was talking about the ideological persona. Human personas across the world want the same things, including food, shelter, warmth, security, love, family, friendships, etc. Ideological personas do not. That is the crux of the matter.

Human Bonds and Ideological Diversity

With the two personas in our vocabulary, we now have a way to address these differences without reducing one to the other. We can use our shared humanity to create strong bonds, tend to each other's basic needs, and affirm that we all belong to the human tribe. At the same time, we need to allow for ideological diversity and maintain the ability to discuss ideological differences without seeing them as an attack on the human persona.

PERSONAL INITIATIVES

Shared Human Elements

Make a list of the elements that you share with every other human being on this planet. Write everything that comes to mind and then add to your list every time you encounter something new that is distinctly human. Having such a catalog will accomplish two things. First, you will be looking for what you have in common with people you encounter. Second, an ever-growing list of shared characteristics will strengthen the bonds you feel with the rest of humanity. It will remind you that even though we may belong to different tribes due to family, geography, interests, and ideology, we all belong to the larger tribe of humanity.

Unmask Your Ideological Persona

Unmask your ideological persona by listing everything that you believe and value. Examine the labels you use to define yourself and explore the differences between empirically provable facts and your chosen beliefs. Plato extolled the virtues of living an examined life. Too many people parrot their beliefs and values without ever taking a closer look. Their ideological persona has come together almost through happenstance. Unmasking what you believe and where those beliefs came from can be an eye-opening experience—even for those who have chosen their beliefs carefully.

Rethink Your Use of Ideological Labels

Language is labeler-in-chief. Simply pointing to something and identifying it with a word is an act of labeling. As such, labels (however incomplete) are helpful shortcuts. They allow humans to communicate about everything from nuanced physical science to emotional states and abstract ideas.

Nothing wrong with that. Not all labels are bad.

However, it's the excessive and aggressive ideological labeling that deepens divides. With that in mind, rethink your use. Examine when labeling helps and when it hurts. Have you, for instance, ever used labels to describe another person and later found out that you were wrong? What did that feel like and how did it change your thinking? What about the opposite, that is, other people labeling you and being wrong? What did that feel like?

There is a time and place to employ labels in our communications, but when we are dealing with ideological differences, it can be helpful to slow down, ask questions, and consider nuance rather than paint everything black and white with simple narratives and easy to apply stickers.

Imagine

What would human persona focused politics look like?

3. The Importance of Shared Human Experiences

The reason for participating in shared human experiences is fairly simple. If people can be around each other doing human things—i.e., things that everyone does, such as eating food, helping others, creating, talking about their family, sharing their life story, etc. —and not feel threatened, then anxieties are reduced, empathy is increased, trust is built, and perceptions are changed.

My Experience with Interfaith Events

My experience with all types of interfaith events has underscored the importance of human-to-human interactions. Due to my active engagement, I have had an opportunity to spend time with people of all faiths —which here means all strongly held beliefs, since atheists, humanists and those who call themselves spiritual-but-not-religious also attend these events, albeit in smaller numbers. In hindsight, I can safely say that my involvement has changed my perceptions more than I expected. Every time I drive home from one of these events, a sense of connectedness lingers, subtle anxieties that I didn't know existed about visual or ideological differences have been reduced, my ability to empathize with those who espouse different beliefs has increased, and I feel more hopeful about the human race.

One would think that something amazing would need to have taken place to create such fantastic results or that I was somehow special in my ability to relate with others. Neither is true. Interactions during these interfaith gatherings are usually rather mundane. In fact, what is unique about them is their mundaneness.

Imagine going to an event with a sense of trepidation, thinking that everyone there is going to be completely different from you. Initially, you would only see those differences, including different garbs and religious wear, different races, different accents, and so on.

However, as you begin to mingle and interact, you find more and more similarities. Little by little you realize that all the people there are related through universal shared humanity. They eat like you, laugh like you, think about the weather in the same way, talk about their feelings, share stories about their families, feel the need for safety, and down the list you go. The experience is ordinary but life-changing at the same time.

Anxiety, Trust, Empathy, and Perceptions

I've used four words to underscore the importance of shared human experiences: trust, empathy, perceptions, and anxiety. Allow me to offer more detailed definitions, starting with the Merriam-Webster dictionary designations:

- *Anxiety:* Apprehensive uneasiness or nervousness, usually over an impending or anticipated ill.
- *Trust*: Reliance on the character, ability, strength, or truth of someone or something.
- *Empathy*: The action of understanding, being aware of, being sensitive to, and vicariously experiencing the feelings, thoughts, and experiences of another.
- *Perception*: A capacity for comprehension, a mental image.

When people feel anxiety, it revolves around an anticipated ill. Anticipation requires imagination, which means that feelings of anxiety arise because of an imagined outcome based on the information that we have already gathered through our perception. When the information is wrong or our perception limited (prejudiced) we experience unnecessary anxiety. For example, if you've never met a person of a particular faith or ideological disposition, then all you have to go on is your imagination and that is limited by your experiences, conversations, and quite often colored by the news or images you gather. Since news outlets primarily focus on the disruption of harmony, they serve as an unreliable source that can easily increase anxiety.

This is why anxiety and perceptions go hand in hand. In the same way that we need to taste a variety of fruits and sugary products to pinpoint the concept of sweetness, we need to interact with a variety of people to perceive our sense of shared humanity. Once we are able to modify our perceptions through direct interactions, we reduce levels of anxiety because we no longer anticipate based on incomplete information.

On the topic of trust, most people have developed fairly acute ways to measure trust and honesty in personal interactions. It's not an exact science and some people are better at it than others, but, in general, human beings have the ability to read body language, tone of voice, use of words, and more to gauge whether or not a person is being truthful. While measuring truthfulness and trustworthiness is never easy, it is substantially easier to do through personal interactions than from afar. For instance, how many times have you heard someone say: "This man seems nice enough, but I'll have to meet him in person to see whether or not I can trust him." That is how direct shared human experiences can influence trust or lack thereof.

Finally, to be able to empathize, we have to attempt to see the world from other people's perspectives. We may never be able to know exactly how another person feels, but we can come close by trying to see the world through their eyes. It goes without saying that it's easier to imagine interior sensations after we've had face-to-face encounters. Looking at a picture or reading someone's story can certainly be helpful—and I encourage that type of empathizing—but nothing substitutes direct human-to-human contact.

What Kind of Experiences?

Once we've recognized the importance of engaging in shared human experiences, we need to decide what type of interactions we want to participate in or facilitate. As previously stated, shared human experiences can revolve around anything that brings people together at the human level; in essence, events where human personas can interact without being forced to either defend or disseminate ideological viewpoints.

I used to think that going to events where the main goal was to mingle and get to know the everyday aspects of other people's lives was a waste of time. My goal was always to get into deep ideological conversations where I could either resonate with people's ideas or prod them to explain or defend their points of view. While I still enjoy interesting ideological discussions, I was wrong to dismiss commonplace human elements. Exploring our shared humanity is never a waste of time. In fact, it seems to be the only doorway that will open up a possibility for respectful ideological exchanges.

On the following pages, I will provide several examples of shared human encounters, many of which can be done in a socially distanced way without losing their essence. Hopefully, this list will get you started. Just remember that getting people together is a creative process and that the only thing that limits your options is your own imagination.

Eating Together

Breaking bread. Sitting down for a meal together. These are probably the oldest forms of human experience. We all need to eat, so why not use that time to connect with other people? Meals have been used to broker peace during times of war, settle personal disputes, reconnect estranged family members, deepen romantic connections, create strong business alliances, fan the embers of love, and much more.

Food can be central in our efforts to create shared human experiences. Even when that is not the focal point, it's always a good idea to feed people when they come together. More than ninety percent of the interreligious, interfaith, and interideological events that I have attended have included food as a major component.

Doing Good Works Together

Imagine this. You are working at a food drive to help the less fortunate. You look to one side and find someone of a different faith. You look to the other side and find someone of a different political persuasion. You realize that none of that matters. You are doing good works side-by-side and understand that helping people is the only reason why all of you have come together.

Whatever the project, there is something magical that happens when people focus on helping others. The poet, Rabindranath Tagore, explained the essence of service orientation eloquently when he wrote:

"I slept and dreamt that life was joy.
I awoke and saw that life was service.
I acted and behold, service was joy."

Worshipping and Meditating Together

While interfaith and interreligious events focus on improving relations between people with strong differing beliefs, multifaith spaces have been popping up all over the world. The goal of these spaces is to allow people to worship, pray, and meditate side-by-side. While each person stays within the realm of his or her own faith tradition (ideology), the activity offers an opportunity to observe shared humanity in action, everything from personal peace and quiet to feelings of elation, quiet sobbing, and sincerity. Emotions and physical behaviors have the potential to trigger shared human resonance in others who are in the space.

Learning Together

Elementary schools, high schools, and college campuses offer unique opportunities to interact with people of all faiths and persuasions, even more so than workplaces. On average, intermingling is more active when kids are younger and becomes more difficult as the ideological persona grows stronger and beliefs solidify. Organizations such as Interfaith Youth Core and Convergence on Campus have done a great job of facilitating relationships between students in higher learning environments, but more can be done so that people don't automatically segregate into ideological camps.

For the average adult, attending seminars, workshops, and other forms of adult education can create interesting connections between people who wouldn't normally socialize but have similar interests. As a veteran workshop and seminar facilitator, I can tell you that the connections made are often more important than the material being presented.

Engaging in Small Talk

Ordinary conversations can be used to deepen shared human connections. For that to happen, the exchanges simply need to be empathetic and revolve around features that we all share as human beings, including lifecycle, health, emotions, kids, work, housing situation, commuting, weather, feelings, entertainment, food, travel, pets, hobbies, family history... or something similar. I know that I am suggesting small talk and that I shouldn't have to mention it, but, in our age of ideological overemphasizing, we need to remind ourselves of the importance of everyday discussions that people used to take for granted.

Exploring Human Interconnectedness

This one can be done alone or in a group. Take manmade items and wonder how many people it took to create them. Objects of focus can be anything, a pen, table, sandwich, computer, book, or something else. The idea is to contemplate every part of the construction, from the extraction or creation of building materials to the manufacturing and distribution process. In my house, we sometimes play this game at the dinner table and it is astounding to realize how many people have come together to make it possible for us to have a meal. From a single man-made object, we can truly realize that we are never alone and that all human beings are linked and indebted to their natural environment.

Creating Together

Art offers a unique way to connect with the creative aspect of being human. From flash orchestras for peace (which is a real thing) to pottery and painting, artistic experiences plug into an important element. All kids are creative until the day that some are told that they are artists and others are told they are no good. Yet, for those who are not artists, the need for creativity is still there. If we give rise to creativeness in a safe environment and invite people from a variety of backgrounds to join in, the outcome can be magical.

Reading About Others

Not everyone has a chance to interact with diverse groups of people. In some cases, the limitations are geographical, other times people don't have the time —and then there's the pandemic. With that in mind, reading memoirs and biographies with an emphasis on shared humanity can create a special kind of bond. The same can be said about blogs that focus on every-day life and are not heavy on ideology. Empathy is elicited when you see how much you have in common with the person you are reading about, even though the two of you are worlds apart.

Exercising Together

In his book, *The Blue Zones*, Dan Buettner presents findings about health and longevity from communities around the world. One of the insights is that commu-nal exercising, such as walking or running in groups where the physical exercise is supplemented with personal interactions, has more positive impacts on health than merely exercising alone.

Playing Games

"Man is man's joy" is a proverb from the *Poetic Edda* that I heard repeated over and over again during my childhood in Iceland. Human beings seek each other's company. Playing games is probably the oldest pastime in our collective history. From physically active sports to card games and strategy, there is great variety in this field of human endeavor. For the purposes of engaging shared humanity, age-appropriate and mostly good-natured games need to be chosen, since we don't want to feed the competitive spirit too much and create a new type of divide. The overarching intention is to connect one human persona with another. This may sound simplistic to some, but if people with differing worldviews can play games and laugh a little in each other's company that opens the door for other and more meaningful interactions. Trust is built slowly. Sometimes the first step is to see a glimpse of shared humanity.

Other Experiences

The above examples only scratch the surface of what can be done in the name of shared human experiences. Use your creativity to come up with more ideas.

If You Decide to Facilitate

You can join others who are already facilitating groups around one or more of these activities or you can decide to create your own group. If you decide to facilitate, remember that you are creating an ideology-free-zone. No politics, religion, or other ideologies are allowed. This is difficult to achieve but of utmost importance. The primary objective is to allow for human-to-human contact. As we've explored, such interactions have the potential to break down barriers and build trust. However, even if none of that is achieved, the mere act of being in each other's presence (so long as it is non-threatening) can have an energetic impact. There is nothing spooky about it; we feel the presence of others. Face-to-face meetings can achieve results that can never be achieved through other means. Our overarching purpose may be to reduce anxiety, increase trust, elicit empathy, and change perceptions, but we will gladly settle for an outcome where two or more people who disagree with each other have spent time in the same space without behaving like enemies.

PERSONAL INITIATIVES

Participate in Shared Human Experiences

Participate (safely) in as many shared human experiences as you can. Be around people who have different ideological preferences while doing things that underline your shared humanity. Use every chance you get to connect through shared humanity and see where it leads.

Walk a Mile...

Make an effort to walk a mile in other people's shoes, especially when you disagree with them. Try to see their daily lives as if they were your own.

List Your Ideas for Experiential Events

The ideas we have explored thus far only denote a micro-particle of what is possible. Unleash your imagination and list all the ideas that you have for shared human experiences.

4. Engaging in Structured Dialogue

There are four primary reasons to engage in structured dialogue: (1) Relate with people at a human level, (2) learn about similarities and differences, (3) persuade others, and (4) resolve conflicts, which, depending on their severity, can often benefit from the help of a mediator.

Public Monologues

In the public arena, we have plenty of clashes about ideological differences. Citizens, politicians, pundits, and religious leaders try to convince people left and right. Sadly, most of those interactions suffer from a similar malady. People are not listening. Instead, they are launching ideological monologues, or worse, trying to land insults that will make them look good in the eyes of their ideological tribe. While we need to have clear-eyed discussions about matters that influence everyone's lives and find a balance between freedom to do what we want and responsibility towards those who share the planet with us, no conversation is to be had until we are willing to listen.

The Importance of Dialogue

It can be hard to see the importance of being exposed to ideas that don't rhyme with our own, especially when we live in a society where most people identify with their chosen ideology and channel much of their online activity through a lens of beliefs and values. And yet, dialogue has proven itself to be the least intrusive and most constructive way to engage with another human being. From early in life, most people are taught to use their words, not their fists, which is a fitting guideline for people who seek common ground. If you find yourself resisting dialogue—something I've had to contend with from time to time—remind yourself that if escalation were the answer, we would already be moving in the right direction.

Laying the Foundation for Dialogue

Well-meaning people often rush into ideological dialogue about differences and grievances prematurely without doing the necessary foundation work. Keep in mind that sincere dialogue can only take place when people have begun to trust and respect each other. For that to happen, they need to see each other as equally human. There is no way around it. Instead of jumping right into dialogue, remember to grease the wheels with shared human experiences first, such as the ones proposed in the previous chapter. The mere act of eating together before a dialogue can be enough to allow people to see glimpses of shared humanity.

Why Use Structured Guidelines?

When I introduce the importance of structured dialogue guidelines in my workshops, I sometimes get pushback. "Why can't we just talk to each other?" people ask. My answer is simple. There is a time and place for unstructured dialogue and if it happens naturally, simply go with the flow, but sitting people down in a circle, by a table, or facing each other—strangers, who have little in common—and asking them to engage in unstructured dialogue about something, anything, is a recipe for disaster. Structure allows people to create mutual agreements, set clear agendas, generate a conciliatory tone, have time limits, and more. As such, structure is as important to dialogue as plates and silverware are to fine dining.

Focus on Learning and Sharing

Of the four types of dialogue mentioned earlier, dialogue that is focused on learning and sharing has proven to be the most effective way to find common ground. It's an approach that encourages the creation of no-pressure zones and gives people exposure to a variety of different perspectives without generating a feeling that they have to change their core beliefs or

values. On the following pages, I will present five test-
ed and proven types of interideological dialogue
guidelines that all focus on learning and sharing. Sub-
sequently, we will look at persuasion and conflict resolution.

The Red Bench™ Agreement

My exposure to interfaith dialogue has mainly come
through my involvement with iACT (Interfaith Action
of Central Texas) whose volunteers have trained me to
be a table host at their Red Bench interfaith dialogue
events. Being a host is different from being a facilitator
because a host takes part in the discussion instead of
directing the process like a neutral observer. At our
monthly events, we've discussed topics such as love,
hope, home, divine presence, justice, and more. The
following is our agreement for a great conversation.

- Open-mindedness: Listen to and respect all points
  of view.
- Acceptance: Suspend judgment as best you can.
- Curiosity: Seek to understand rather than persuade; we are not here to "fix" one another.
- Discovery: Question old assumptions, look for new
  insights.
- Sincerity: Speak to yourself, from your heart, about
  what has personal meaning to you.
- Brevity: Go for honesty and depth but don't go on
  and on.

When everyone accepts these boundaries, the conversation goes well. I have yet to attend a Red Bench dialogue that veered off track. That is thanks to our pledge (above), scripted guidelines (which all table hosts follow), the training that we receive, and sincere attendees.

Respectful Conversations

The Minnesota Council of Churches created similar guidelines for their Respectful Conversations initiative.

1. Speak for yourself
2. Practice respect
3. Be brief
4. Listen carefully
5. Respect confidentiality
6. Allow people to pass

If you are interested in seeing a demonstration, the Theater of Public Policy created a short video to illustrate these guidelines. You can find it on YouTube.

Experifaith Dialogue

In my 2017 book, titled *Experifaith: At the Heart of Every Religion*, I explored experiential similarities between religions and urged people to participate in dialogues about their spiritual practices, such as prayer, meditation, worship, service, and more. Here are the dialogue guidelines as they appear in my book.

The Experifaith Agreement:

- We are willing to share and listen, not preach or be preached to.
- We are willing to converse on an experiential level.
- We are committed to being cordial in our interactions.
- We will work in harmony towards a better understanding.

Before the dialogue begins, I usually read the following passage from Gandhi, but you should feel free to choose a passage that has a similar meaning or create your own invocation.

"I offer you peace. I offer you love. I offer you friendship. I see your beauty. I hear your need. I feel your feelings. My wisdom flows from the Highest Source. I salute that source within you. Let us work together for unity and love."

The Experifaith Dialogue Process:

- Please limit discussions to how spiritual experiences have influenced your feelings, thoughts, and/or actions.
- Please refrain from talking about the contents of your belief system, i.e., history, dogma, or orthodoxy. Focus on personal practices and resulting experiences.
- Explore both similarities and differences.

- Another person's experience cannot be wrong, just different. Even if you find nothing in common with another person, the mere act of trying to understand will reap benefits.
- Signal each other by raising your hand if discussions start to revolve around theology rather than experiences

These types of experiential conversations create a sense of shared humanity. For example, when two people of different faiths talk about the power of prayer in their lives and how the practice has influenced them experientially, they are bound to find similarities. This approach is not meant to belittle obvious differences between religious traditions—such as the content of prayers or whom they are directed at—but rather highlight the fact that while stories and customs vary, human experiences are much the same around the globe.

Counterintuitive Secrets

The following is a list of counterintuitive secrets from the book *Circles of Men* by Clay Boykin. In his research, Clay found that many groups failed because they were too rigid, their language was overly structured, and nobody wanted to be fixed. His goal was to create heart-centered connections where men felt safe. Here are some of his secrets along with short explanations.

- Language Matters: Words are at the center of these guidelines.
- Framework but Very Little Structure: A rough framework allows participants to decouple from their organized daily lives.
- Network instead of Group: Networks are open and fluid while groups tend to be closed.
- Intention instead of Commitment: Intention signifies energized focus rather than an unyielding pledge.
- Gathering instead of Meeting: Nothing needs to get done or be decided upon when participants are gathering.
- Facilitating instead of Leading: The facilitator is not the leader.
- Heart over Head: Participants are given permission to release control and move into their hearts.
- Conversation instead of Discussion: Having a discussion connotes a conclusion, participants are instead having an open-ended conversation.
- Holding Space instead of Fixing: Participants listen to affirm one another with compassion without offering similar stories or trying to fix one another.

These secrets are intentionally vague to allow for interpretation, but they convey an overarching sensibility that can be applied to a variety of dialogue situations.

Your Choices Reflect Your Goals

All of these guidelines share several similarities. They call for mutual respect, the development of trust, time limits, and brevity in interactions, creating room for genuine connections, encouraging authentic communications from a personal or experiential standpoint, and honoring the fact that human beings have two ears and one mouth.

The differences between them are also numerous and largely depend on the reason for gathering. Some are flexible while others are rigid, some ask a lot of participants while others ask a little, some are focused on shared humanity while others explore ideological distinctions, and so on.

When you choose your approach, make sure that it is in line with the goals that you have set for your gathering. In preparation, ask these questions: Do we want participants to stay on the surface and focus on cordial co-human interactions or to go deep and explore shared experiences? Is our primary goal to create trust between people or explore differences (maybe both)? Do we want the conversation to be light and inspiring or do we want to address wounds that need healing?

Your answers will help you to set the tone for your gathering and assist you in deciding which dialogue guidelines to follow.

The Ratio Between Listening and Talking

In their talks, the three Interfaith Amigos—Imam Jamal Rahman, Pastor Don Mackenzie, and Rabbi Ted Falcon—provide a comical reenactment of their first encounters by talking over each other. "My scripture this, my tradition that..." was pretty much all they could say to each other in the beginning. However, their relationship began to improve significantly when they started listening deeply. Now they travel the world and convey lessons that they have learned from their interactions, the most important of which is to listen. In our search for common ground, listening and learning about the other comes first while sharing comes second.

Listening is crucial

I'll admit that this focus on listening has been extremely difficult for me. I still haven't mastered the two ears to one mouth ratio, probably because I have been a public speaker for most of my adult life and I usually have something to say. I am aware of this shortcoming and practice listening every chance I get. Asking questions is the most potent tool at my disposal. It has also been tremendously helpful to be vulnerable about my tendency and catch myself publicly when I stray off track by saying something like, "Oops! There I go again," which has the added benefit of being a confusing reference to two popular songs.

I share this personal admission to underscore the importance of self-awareness and practice. Even with the best of intentions, all of us can fall into familiar patterns during conversations. Our attempt to apply unfamiliar dialogue principles takes practice and sincere willingness. Whenever I am tempted to appear perfect in my interactions with others, I remind myself of this passage by David D. Burns, one of the pioneers of cognitive-behavioral therapy:

"Aim for success, not perfection. Never give up your right to be wrong, because then you will lose the ability to learn new things and move forward with your life. Remember that fear always lurks behind perfectionism. Confronting your fears and allowing yourself the right to be human can, paradoxically, make yourself a happier and more productive person."

Sincere Dialogue Facilitation

The guidelines for facilitating dialogue are similar to the guidelines for facilitating shared human experiences. Set an intention, be well prepared, outline the agreement (dialogue guidelines), stay on topic, and respect time limits. Overall, participants can be passionate, introverted, curious, seemingly uninterested, and everything in between. Don't dismiss anyone. Your role is not to make judgments about participants, but allow them to share and keep the conversation going. Direct contact with many personality types is just as important as exposure to many points of view. Give people space to make up their own minds about what they have seen and heard. Dialogue facilitation should focus on the creation of safe spaces where people feel that they can open up and share with each other.

That said, facilitators don't have to be perfect. If you are facilitating dialogue and you mess up, you mess up. Say you're sorry and move on. Instead of aiming for perfection, strive for sincerity.

What If You Want to Persuade?

What if you disagree vehemently with another person? What can you do to make them see things your way? The short answer to that question is: Nothing. You can't make anyone do anything, least of all change his or her mind.

However, if you earnestly want to persuade someone, here are several insights from Megan Phelps-Roper who gave an instructional TED talk about her shift away from extremism. She was raised in the Westboro Baptist Church, which, for those who don't know, is a controversial church that exults in demonizing those who don't follow the word of God (her description). Her earliest memory of the church's activism was when she was five years old, standing on a street corner in Kansas holding a sign that read: "Gays are worthy of death."

I will not recount her entire story in this book—her TED talk is riveting and well worth your time—but it suffices to say that through persistent online interactions with people who disagreed with her, she changed her mind, left the church, and now works as a writer and educator on topics related to extremism, bullying, and empathy. To better understand why and how she changed her mind, she unveiled four things that the people who persuaded her did differently and now presents them as guidelines for others. The following is my slightly rephrased version.

- Don't assume bad intent: Even when people are professing to ideologies that you vigorously disagree with, assume that they are trying to do the right thing in the best way they know how. Supposing bad intent makes us forget our shared humanity and cuts off the possibility for understanding.
- Ask questions: Effective counterarguments cannot be made unless there is an understanding of where the other side is coming from. Asking questions helps us map the disconnect and signals to the other person that he or she is being heard.
- Stay calm: As you can imagine, staying calm takes practice and patience. Tell a joke, excuse yourself from the conversation, take a deep breath, but refuse to escalate.
- Make the argument: People who have strong beliefs often assume that the value of their position is obvious and self-evident. We need to be willing to make the argument for our point of view instead of presenting our preferred ideology as fact

When it works—and let me restate that it infrequently does—persuasion is a gentle and patient art rather than a bulldozer. Too many people are engaged in head-on collisions these days. Using this tempered approach to persuasion is a step in the right direction. Just remember that the ideological persona can make argument after argument without making a dent in another person's thinking unless the human persona has been engaged in a meaningful way. Remarkably enough, Megan Phelps-Roper's humanity was engaged in the digital space, showing that it is possible to be co-human there, even though it is harder to do than in face-to-face meetings.

With all of that being said, I have long lived by the words of author and motivational speaker Dale Carnegie, who said that:

"A man convinced against his will, is of the same opinion still."

I usually back off when I meet strong ideological resistance in someone I don't know. The reason? I have not had a chance to engage his or her human persona successfully. Based on my experience, no one will get convinced of anything except his or her own righteousness if an argument keeps intensifying. Incessantly pressing my point could endanger a later opportunity to engage with the human persona in my ideological opponent—maybe forever.

As much as people would like to believe that everyone can be persuaded like Megan Phelps-Roper was, persuasion usually doesn't come from the outside. Whether you are a Zen trainee, corporate board member, religious zealot, or political activist, change usually comes from the inside. For illustration, it's good to remember that an eggshell broken from the outside signals destruction while an eggshell broken from the inside denotes the beginning of a new life.

People Listen To...

The greatest lesson I've learned from being involved in interfaith dialogue is simple: People are most likely to listen to others that they already know and respect. Always keep that in mind.

Resolving Differences

People have disagreements. That's just the way life is. Individuals fight, families fight, neighbors fight, countries fight… and on it goes. And yet, even though the desire for vengeance is automatic and animalistic, the behavior that makes human beings unique is our capacity for forgiveness. Forgiveness requires real thought-out action that releases both the forgiver and the forgiven. It is miracle-like in its ability to transform worldly situations and nullify past actions. Thusly, according to our new narrative, forgiveness is an essential element of the soul-force, without which we, as a people, would perish.

When I was researching for this project, I visited a professor at a nearby college that teaches mediation. I was hoping to get access to tricks-of-the-trade that I could share with my readers. What I found was a nuanced field that relies heavily on skill and training. There are no universal tips that can be applied to every situation.

That being said, I did garner two insights from the professor that I thought worth sharing.

a) When seeking solutions, try to put aside personalities and history. Focus instead on facts and competing interests. It is much easier to talk about the issues than argue for or against subjective likability or be preoccupied with a past that cannot be changed. Temperaments and preceding events tend to ignite passions rather than reason.

b) Dive deeper into competing interests by asking the question: What do they actually want? The professor offered me an example. He asked me to imagine that I have two kids (which I do) and that both of them wanted the last orange in the house. The quick and easy way to resolve that situation would be to cut the orange in half and be done with it. But, he said, a mediator takes time to dig deeper. If, for example, the parent finds out that one kid needs the orange peel for a cake recipe and the other needs the orange seeds for a growing experiment, then cutting the orange in half would serve neither. In fact, by looking deeper, the parent can give both kids precisely what they are looking for.

Make a Commitment to Dialogue

Whether you intend to connect through discussions about similar experiences, learn and share, gently persuade, or resolve differences, I urge you to make a commitment to dialogue. Of all the options we have for finding common ground, dialogue still reigns supreme as a method for connection and conflict resolution.

PERSONAL INITIATIVES

Use Dialogue Guidelines With Friends

Try using some of the previously mentioned dialogue guidelines in conversations with your friends and acquaintances before you attempt to use them in larger settings. Choose appropriate guidelines, make an agreement, discuss a topic, and then review the process to see what went well and what you struggled with. Examine the process and evaluate it for yourself. Once you feel comfortable, you can use the same guidelines with strangers in more diverse situations.

Attend Dialogue Sessions (if available)

Densely populated areas in the USA usually offer some sort of interfaith or interreligious dialogue programs and you should be able to find what you are looking for with a simple Internet search. For those who live away from urban areas, smaller interideological programs are being run across the country, and you may find one in your area. It can be quite daunting to enter this realm for the first time. Attend with an open mind and see what you find.

Don't Take Words Too Personally

Dialogue is hard enough without people being too sensitive. It goes without saying that most aggressive forms of name-calling and labeling should be confronted, but refrain from misinterpreting people's words and gestures as insults. Offer gentle feedback instead of responding with indignation. Most of all, give people the benefit of the doubt.

Create Your Own Guidelines

Make a list of all the elements that you deem important from the guidelines offered in this book and use them as inspiration to create your own dialogue guidelines. This exercise can inform your approach to interactions in the future and give you a sense of what is important to you in structured settings, even if you never use your method to orchestrate a dialogue of your own.

To Host or Not to Host?

Should you host a dialogue session or not? That depends. Do you have a burning desire? Do you have access to space? Are there enough people in your circle of influence to generate interest? I've heard of successful dialogue programs that were launched through Meetup.com and some that started in living rooms. Inversely, I've heard of unsuccessful programs that were initiated by large organizations that had not done the necessary footwork to prepare.

5. Being the Change

There are many things we can do to find common ground and further the cause of social harmony. However, before we can harmonize with others, we must first tune our own instruments.

"If we could change ourselves, the tendencies in the world would also change. As a man changes his own nature, so does the attitude of the world change towards him. We need not wait to see what others do."

This Mohandas Mahatma Gandhi quote was later shortened, supposedly by his grandson, Arun Gandhi, into the better known:

"Be the change you want to see in the world."

Both versions point to a great truth.

All outer work begins within. If we are to influence the world around us, even in minor ways, the real work begins inside and emanates outwards. We don't need to be perfect to do good deeds in the world, but we need to be sincere in our efforts. People who are in continual states of discord (i.e., outraged, negative, demanding, judgmental, spiteful, etc.) while they try to promote bridge-building and common ground are bound to fail.

To paraphrase Emerson, 'how people act speaks so loudly that we can't hear what they are saying.' For best results, harmony should resonate from within, and an alignment of thought, word, and deed is preferable.

From Self-Care to World-Care

Carol Gilligan's model for moral development shows that human beings generally move from being selfish to being able to care for others in their near environment to, in rare cases, showing genuine care for people they don't know (here, care is defined as an action, not merely a nice thought). When we compare her model to others in the same vein—including Piaget, Loevinger, Erikson, Steiner, Beck, Graves, Kohlberg, Peck, Fowler, Wilber, and others—moral growth corresponds with people's ability to see the world from an ever-increasing number of perspectives and act accordingly; a classification that rhymes with compassion, defined as the sympathetic consciousness of others' distress together with a desire to alleviate it. Simply put, moral growth leads to increased compassion and care.

Let's take a brief look at the progression from selfish to care to world-care.

At stage one, a person that is selfish can only see the world from his or her point of view. The healthy version of selfishness produces self-care and win-win situations while the unhealthy version produces battles and win-lose scenarios, where selfish desires are achieved at other people's expense. Society has a number of names for the latter, including narcissism, vanity, egotism, and self-absorption.

At the second stage, care, individuals become generous towards those who are within their circle of care, including spouses, family, friends, and near community. A person that has begun to care for another is willing to sacrifice time, energy, and money unselfishly so that another may grow and flourish (M. Scott Peck's definition of love). The ability to care for others epitomizes the underpinnings of civilized society. Without a tapestry of caring, civilization would collapse into a chaotic every-man-for-himself battlefield.

The third stage of development, world-care, is relatively uncommon. It depends on people's ability to show care (take action) for others they do not know. World-care can start with minor things, such as a genuine willingness to pay taxes for the greater good or reducing personal consumption to curb carbon emissions, but, as empathy grows, people at the stage of world-care will genuinely attempt to care for everyone, often at their own expense.

Expanding the Circle of Care

If individuals want to increase their aptitude for care and compassion, they need to establish self-care and then expand their abilities outwards. The most common metaphors are: learn how to swim before you attempt to rescue a drowning person, when pressure falls in an airplane cabin, put the oxygen mask on yourself first and then on your child, you have to earn money before you can give money, and demonstrate love for those who are near you before you attempt to love the entire world. The underlying principle is always the same. Caring is an ability. If you cannot care for yourself, how can you care for others? Expanding the circle of care looks something like this:

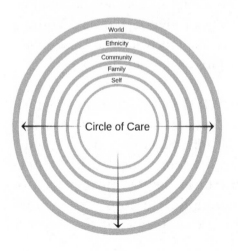

Each successive circle denotes an increased ability to care for more and more people. Let's take a look at four examples of this behavior, including Gandhi, Mother Teresa, Nelson Mandela, and Betty Williams, three of whom won the Nobel Peace Prize and one who deserved to but was never awarded.

India's Great Soul

Mohandas Mahatma Gandhi (1869-1948) was a towering figure in history. He lived his philosophy of non-violent resistance (satyagraha) to the best of his ability. His approach, which grew into a full-fledged ideology with many specific tenets, was primarily based on acts of self-control, developing peace from within, and standing firm when it came to righteous convictions, never at the expense of others but always at one's own expense. He preached that satyagrahis should never hate the doer, only resist the action, and that no human being was beyond redemption, repeatedly stating that:

"It is easy enough to be friendly to one's friends. But to befriend the one who regards himself as your enemy is the quintessence of true religion. The other is mere business."

As a lawyer, activist, spiritual figure, and politician, Gandhi was not beyond reproach, but looking at his life, one can hardly doubt the sincerity of his convictions nor argue against their effectiveness.

His road from self-care to world-care began with a spiritual upbringing in India and a legal education in England, both of which became central to his later work. Pride was the seed that flowered into a lifetime of activism. After buying a first-class train ticket via mail, Gandhi was thrown out of his prepaid cabin and off the train, merely for being an Indian. That incident so insulted his dignity, that he went to work for the civil rights of the Indian community in South Africa. It was there, with inspiration from Thoreau, among others, that he developed his philosophy of nonviolent civil disobedience.

After success in South Africa, Gandhi returned to India and expanded his circle of care to include the Indian people who quickly bestowed on him the honorary title Mahatma, which means Great (Maha) Soul (Atman). He spent most of his adult life working towards Indian independence at a tremendous personal expense. Sacrifice was really at the heart of his philosophy; the will to suffer until the suffering became unbearable in the eyes of the oppressors.

Partly thanks to his efforts, India finally gained independence in 1947, one year prior to his assassination. In the final year of his life, Gandhi felt a deep need to expand his circle of care to include all of the world's inhabitants and was increasingly worried about world peace, but, since his life was cut short, we will never know what kind of work he would have engaged in.

Today, Gandhi is a revered historical figure, sometimes to the point of deification (especially in India), but he was simultaneously an exceptional servant of humanity and a flawed human being. He readily admitted to some of those flaws in his autobiography while other shortcomings have been exposed in the light of modern values.

What we can surmise from Gandhi's story is this. Without a modicum of self-care—including a spiritual upbringing and high-quality education—he would not have been prepared to fill his role of service and would likely have failed. Personal pride may have been the instigator for his activism, but he grew into the role and became more selfless with every passing year. His vocation required tremendous sacrifices, especially in regards to his family, as Gandhi spent much of his adult life in and out of prison. His expansion was realized step-by-step by living an intentional life focused on service.

From Housewife to Nobel Laureate

Betty Williams (1943) was a fierce proponent of peace in Northern Ireland during the Troubles and won the Nobel Peace Prize in 1976 for co-founding Community of Peace People with Mairead Corrigan and Ciaran McKeown.

There was no shortage of violence in Northern Ireland during the conflict, but the breaking point for

Williams and her co-founders was when three children, Joanne (eight-years-old), John (two-and-a-half-years-old), and Andrew (six-weeks-old), were killed during a high-speed chase in West Belfast.

Imagine that. A young mother was walking her kids down the street on a bright sunny afternoon, her youngest in a stroller, her toddler walking by her side, and her daughter riding a bicycle. Soldiers shot a fleeing man dead and his car plowed into the children outside of St. John the Baptist School. Although Ann Maguire, the mother of the children, survived the incident, it so haunted her that she took her own life three and a half years later.

Betty Williams was a housewife at the time and resonated deeply with this event. She thought of her own children and how tensions were escalating out of control. Emotions welled up inside of her ("This has to stop!") and caused her to take action. Along with her two co-founders, she started walking the streets, knocking on doors, and asking people to sign a petition that called for an end to violence.

The declaration for their organization read:

"We have a simple message to the world from this movement for Peace. We want to live and love and build a just and peaceful society. We want for our children, as we want for ourselves, our lives at home, at work, and at play to be lives of joy and Peace. We recognize that to build such a society demands dedication,

hard work, and courage. We recognize that there are many prob-lems in our society which are a source of conflict and violence. We recognize that every bullet fired and every exploding bomb make that work more difficult. We reject the use of the bomb and the bullet and all the techniques of violence. We dedicate our-selves to working with our neighbors, near and far, day in and day out, to build that peaceful society in which the tragedies we have known are a bad memory and a continuing warning."

People took note. Women flocked to their side. The communal longing for a peaceful resolution was evi-dent. Betty Williams was elevated from housewife to Nobel Peace Prize laureate in a relatively short amount of time.

She attributes the success of her initiative to passion-ate action—which included funneling energy and out-rage into walking door to door, marching, and orga-nizing—but she humbly admits that it was also due to the media attention they got because of a slow news season that summer.

Ever since her work began in Northern Ireland, Williams has been actively expanding her circle of care. She heads the Global Children's Foundation and co-founded the Nobel Women's Initiative in 2006. She lectures widely on topics of peace, education, intercul-tural and interfaith understanding, anti-extremism, and children's rights.

Nun, Teacher, Mother, Saint

Mother Teresa (1910-1997), born Anjezë Gonxhe Bojaxhiu in Albania, is another Nobel Peace Prize laureate (1979) that is worth mentioning in this context.

She left her home in Albania in 1928 to join the Sisters of Loreto in Ireland and become a missionary. That led her to India in 1929 where she taught at St. Teresa's School until she experienced "the call within the call" in 1946, at which time she had been helping the poor while living among them during a retreat. The work for which she is known around the world today began in 1948 and was formally granted permission from the Vatican in 1950 when she founded the Missionaries of Charity. She, along with the sisters in her order, took vows of chastity, poverty, obedience, and wholehearted free service to the poorest of the poor.

The first several years of her work were enormously difficult. She had to beg for food and supplies while experiencing loneliness and a yearning for the comforts of convent life. She wrote in her diary:

"The poverty of the poor must be so hard for them. While looking for a home I walked and walked till my arms and legs ached. I thought how much they must ache in body and soul, looking for a home, food and health. Then, the comfort of Loreto [her former congregation] came to tempt me. "You have only to say the word and all that will be yours again," the Tempter kept

*on saying ... Of free choice, my God, and out of love for you, I
desire to remain and do whatever be your Holy will in my re-
gard. I did not let a single tear come."*

Thanks to her steadfast devotion, the work continued.
She founded hospices where people received medical
attention and were given an opportunity to die with
dignity in accordance with their faith. Muslims were
read the Quran, Hindus received water from the
Ganges, and Catholics received final anointing, all in
accordance with Teresa's belief that no matter their
status in life, people deserved to die like angels—loved
and wanted.

By the 1960s, she had opened orphanages, hospices,
and leper houses throughout India. In 1965, she expanded her congregation abroad and opened a house
in Venezuela with five sisters. Her reach increased
with every passing year, and in 2012 her order had
over 4500 sisters active in 133 countries and was man-
aging homes for people dying of HIV/AIDS, leprosy,
and tuberculosis, and operating soup kitchens, dispen-
saries, mobile clinics, family counseling programs, orphanages, and schools. As her circle of care grew
Teresa proclaimed:

*"By blood, I am Albanian. By citizenship, an Indian. By faith,
I am a Catholic nun. As to my calling, I belong to the world."*

Mother Teresa drew both praise for her work and an
array of criticism—much of which was aimed at her

rigid belief structure. She was canonized in 2016. Today she is known within the Catholic Church as Saint Teresa of Calcutta.

The Prisoner Who Kept an Open Heart

Nelson Mandela (1918-2013) was a complicated man. He trained as a lawyer and openly opposed apartheid (a system of segregation in South Africa that privileged whites). In his early years, Mandela was attracted to Marxism and wanted to engage in nonviolent protests, but he crossed the line into sabotage against the government in 1961 out of frustration. That was one of the factors used against him when he was sentenced to life in prison for conspiring to overthrow the government. Nevertheless, his commitment to democracy was evident, even at his trial, where he said:

"I have fought against white domination, and I have fought against black domination. I have cherished the ideal of a democratic and free society in which all persons will live together in harmony and with equal opportunities. It is an ideal which I hope to live for and to see realized. But if it need be, it is an ideal for which I am prepared to die."

Mandela spent the next twenty-seven years in prison. He wrote his autobiography in secret during that time and garnered support from people all around the world. Outside pressure mounted until he was finally released in 1990.

The most remarkable thing about his story is that he was not consumed with anger, hate, or a need for vengeance after he was set free. Instead, he worked with his oppressors to end apartheid, ran for president of South Africa, and led an unparalleled racial reconciliation process.

Forgiveness is truly the most miraculous aspect of being human. That was certainly the case for Mandela. Seeking revenge would have been most understandable after everything he went through, but he chose to be a unifier instead. He kept his heart open despite a lifetime of adversity. That won him the Nobel Peace Prize in 1993.

After his term as president, Mandela kept on combating poverty and HIV/AIDS through his charitable Nelson Mandela Foundation and worked tirelessly on bringing about peace. In a 2002 Newsweek interview he confessed:

"I really wanted to retire and rest and spend more time with my children, my grandchildren and of course with my wife. But the problems are such that for anybody with a conscience who can use whatever influence he may have to try to bring about peace, it's difficult to say no."

Remarkable Role Models

As I have made clear in this book, I do not believe in perfection. That is why I never put people on pedestals and worship them. Yet, I do see people as role models. I see behaviors that can be replicated. That is what Gandhi, Mother Teresa, Williams, and Mandela are to me. Role models. They weren't flawless, yet they stepped into the public square—where everyone gets criticized, no matter who they are and what they do— and devoted their lives to caring for others in the best ways they knew how. They showed an ability to stay centered during times of tremendous pressure and overcame periods of grief, doubt, and despair with a devotion to causes larger than themselves. Selfish needs were supplanted by selflessness. When they could have stopped, when they could have retired and thought only of themselves, all four continued to work for the benefit of people they did not know because it was the right thing to do.

When I have difficult days of my own, I often think of them and it helps me get back on track. I try to emulate their admirable actions and forgive them for their limitations.

Nurturing Seeds of Care and Compassion

Nurturing basic human decency and empathy has been at the core of all forms of spirituality for millennia. It seems that every religion and moral path has asked adherents to expand their circles of care and develop attitudes of altruism. It's rather amazing when you think about it. Our collective moral evolution has not been dependent on a single ideology or mode of thinking but rather it has bubbled to the surface in all of them. In his classic, *The Varieties of Religious Experience*, William James aptly illustrated that:

"When we survey the whole field of religion, we find a great variety in the thoughts that have prevailed there; but the feelings on the one hand and the conduct on the other are almost always the same, for Stoic, Christian, and Buddhist saints are practically indistinguishable in their lives. The theories which Religion generates, being thus variable, are secondary; and if you wish to grasp her essence, you must look to the feelings and the conduct as being the more constant elements."

His findings need to be underlined. Saints—people who have diligently marched their chosen path to completion—are almost indistinguishable in their lives. Their traditions diverge, both in thought and content, but the outcomes in behavior are amazingly similar. In a religiously pluralistic society, James's conclusions should allay some fears. He is suggesting that the seeds of care and empathy are built into every human being and that a variety of soils and fertilizers will allow those same seeds to grow and flourish. In an ideal world, this would mean that when people devote themselves to their chosen paths with sincerity and intensity and their next-door neighbors do the same, then everyone should eventually meet at the pinnacle of love and compassion... but it doesn't always happen that way, does it? In fact, rigorous adherence to one path often creates disdain for others. Why is that?

Resisting Internal Extremes

Ancient civilizations in the Indus valley made several observations about human nature that still hold true to this day. One of those observations simply stated that when an emotional attraction (raga) to one thing grows, it creates automatic repulsion (dvesha) for the opposite. In short, our like for one thing, instinctively (and often unconsciously) creates a dislike for another. I call this *the attraction-repulsion principle.*

Take dieting as an example. The more you are attracted to healthy foods, the more unhealthy foods disgust you. It's like stretching a rubber band—the stronger the attraction becomes, the stronger your repulsion. If people are moderately attracted to healthy foods, they are moderately repulsed by unhealthy foods. But, once people become 'health nuts'—affectionately called so by others who do not share their strong attraction (wink, wink, nudge, nudge)—they condemn all those who have the occasional candy bar, soda, or fast-food meal and continually rail against sugar- and processed food industries as evil.

Those who have no strong preferences have a difficult time understanding the attraction-repulsion principle. 'Why are these people so upset?' they think to themselves and shrug shoulders. 'I don't get it.'

The answer is simple.

It's because [insert any ideological label] fervently believe in the righteousness of their ideas. It is a tendency that is easy to spot among environmentalists, vegans, political activists, humanists, and is found in some shape or form in every single religious or spiritual environment.

The Seeds are Within

Yet, we should not throw stones in glass houses. This tendency exists in seed form within all of us. The stronger our love for something becomes, the easier it is for us to dislike, despise, or even hate the opposite. In fact, hate and bigotry are often born of good intentions. Love for a nation can turn into hate for another nation; love for the environment can turn into hate of polluters; love for animals can turn into hatred of those who eat them; love for one ideological label can turn into hate for another... and on it goes.

These days, we see this principle very clearly in politics, where people are willing to accuse each other of malevolence just because of differing political ideologies while both sides consider themselves virtuous. The more devoted one side is to their cause, the more they despise the other, which is one reason why extremism is bad for democracy.

Most prominently we see this proclivity in religion. In religion, attraction and repulsion are not merely dependent on personal preferences. Behaviors have been chosen for followers through a combination of religious scriptures and creeds. Devotees are told, in no uncertain terms, what is good and what is evil. Regrettably, such distinctions don't always age well. Rabbi Jonathan Henry Sacks pointed out that each of the world's religions includes "potential minefields" that need to be weeded out, as many religious scriptures offer strong condemnation of women, homosexuality, certain eating habits, types of clothing, and much more. Offenses were (and still are in some places) even punishable by death, which shows an exceptionally strong repulsion. Buddhist philosopher Daisaku Ikeda rightly said that:

"Each religion can be made a force for good or for evil by the people who practice it."

Universal Principle

Like it or not, this built-in propensity is universal among human beings. It is a principle that shows itself throughout. Workshop attendees have told me stories of how strong emotions for nearly everything, including politics, tribal identity, food, drugs, alcohol, and environmental concerns, to name a few, have generated hostile feelings towards people they used to have no problems with.

To my surprise, one participant found the attraction-repulsion principle so repugnant that he condemned my whole program because of it. He believed that I was stuck in the wrong paradigm and that we should move beyond such labels of duality. His words were sharp and his indignation was evident to all. Yet, in all honesty—and because this was an online workshop— we weren't sure whether he was cheekily underscoring the principle or if he was firmly against it.

While some may interpret this ancient observation as black and white, the attraction-repulsion principle exists in shades of gray. The correlation is based on the strength of emotion. Once energy is committed in a single ideological direction, there is a tendency to dismiss, dislike, and eventually become disgusted by the opposite.

For instance, if someone is a fair-weather fan of a sports team, winning and losing mean less to him. The stronger the emotional connection becomes, the more the team's successes and failures influence his life, and the more he allows himself to detest the team's opponents. There is a reason why we see a constant emphasis on sportsmanship in student athletics. It's essentially a warning against the natural inclination towards strong repulsion.

To make this principle even more complicated, there are multitudes of interest and ideologies in life that tug on our emotions. A person can show a moderate temperament in relation to most topics, but then show an exceptionally strong belief for or against something, seemingly out of character. When that happens, we often say that we've 'struck a nerve' on a particular subject.

The gist of it is simple. Strong emotions for something can easily turn into negative attitudes towards the opposite. Cultivation of goodness, kindness, and care can turn into a judgment of opposite behaviors if we are not prudent.

Moderating Behaviors

In general, strong emotional attraction can have many benefits. Austere adherence to everything from dietary rules to moral principles has been shown to deliver positive results. Strong emotions can fire people up and make the 'e' in emotion stand for energy in motion. Groups of people, who have centered their passions on a single mission, are nearly unstoppable. Unwavering beliefs can move mountains. There is a reason why the magnetic pull of emotional attraction has created so many impassioned believers over the millennia.

However, for the sake of social cohesion, people need to keep their love for one thing from turning into hate for another. That is where moderating behaviors come in. They are not meant to moderate attraction or reduce belief, but rather to lessen the likelihood of repulsive obsession, which is a destructive power that can tear through everything from personal relationships to diplomatic relations. There is a big difference between harboring a mild aversion to something and aggressively waging war against ideas and people we don't like.

Although it is quite impossible to quell the human predisposition for repulsion altogether, especially as emotions grow stronger, we can reduce the potential harm. Here are five moderating behaviors that have been known to save people from their own worst instincts:

1. Focus On Attraction: Human beings can only hold a limited number of things in their conscious mind at any one time. We should employ that knowledge to our benefit, for example, by focusing more on behaviors and ideologies that attract us so that there is less mental bandwidth left for something else. Instead of railing against hate, we focus on love; instead of judging the angry, we offer them our peaceful presence; instead of warning against a dystopian future, we provide a hopeful vision. It can be good to be aware of the worst that can happen and be knowledgeable of ideas that are antithetical to harmony, but it is more important to focus on solutions, everything from recognizing shared humanity to learning and sharing through dialogue and developing harmony from within.

2. Be Aware of this Principle: Awareness of the attraction-repulsion principle is often enough to halt the most extreme manifestations. "Whoops. I was so attracted to this idea that I became repulsed by something that didn't use to bother me. Good thing I noticed." This approach is simple enough, but it does require self-awareness.

3. Develop Humility: Humility is advocated in both religion and science. Everyone who pushes their limits, whether they are mental, emotional, intellectual, or spiritual, will find that the more they know, the more they know they don't know. This understanding should lead to humility. Even if we believe in something with our entire being, humility reminds us that, due to the enormity of the universe, there are still many things that we do not and will never know. As Leonard Swidler, professor of interreligious dialogue, is fond of saying: "No one knows everything about anything."

4. Keep Your Sense of Humor: According to research by Dr. Arthur Deikman, religious cults have no sense of humor. Extremism thrives on seriousness. Maintaining the ability to laugh, especially at our own expense, diffuses tension and moderates the repulsive disposition.

5. Slow Down to Understand: In his book, *Thinking, Fast and Slow,* Daniel Kahneman demonstrates how we use our fast-thinking capacity to navigate the world most of the time. Thinking fast is based on our genetic tendencies (collective lessons from navigating the wild, for example), preferred ideologies (confirmation bias, where we look for evidence to confirm what we already believe), labeling (the terms we use to describe our surroundings), and personal experiences, to name a few. In short, thinking fast is like driving a speedy car. Our field of vision narrows the faster we go. While thinking fast can help us in daily life (which is usually somewhat repetitive) it produces severe limits on our capacity when we are faced with unfamiliar circumstances and are trying to find solutions to new problems. Slowing down the thinking process produces better results in those situations. Finding common ground in a diverse world relies on a capacity for slowing down, setting aside our preconceived ideas and initial dislikes, and making an effort to understand 'the other' with nuance. The more you know about what people believe, why they believe it, what motivates them as human beings, and so on, the less likely you are to respond to them with animosity.

Expanding the Circle

Shifting from self-care to world-care is a choice. Those who are willing to grow and actively expand their circle will, (a) use devotion to their chosen spiritual or humanistic tradition to increase capacity for love, care, and compassion, (b) empathize by attempting to understand other people's perspectives, even when they don't agree with them, (c) practice moderating behaviors to stave off natural tendencies towards revulsion that come with increased emotional attraction, (d) beware of the need for perfection, both in themselves and those who they have chosen as their role models, and (e) remember that caring is an act, not merely a feeling. Thomas Merton explained the internal drive toward world-care thusly:

"The whole idea of compassion is based on the keen awareness of the interdependence of all these living beings."

PERSONAL INITIATIVES

Commit to Your Path

To increase your capacity for care, commit to your path. If you are a Christian, Muslim, or Hindu, then be a better Christian, Muslim, or Hindu. If you are a humanist, be a better humanist. If you meditate for peace of mind, devote yourself to your meditation practice. If you serve and volunteer every chance you get, keep doing that with an open heart. As William James concluded, those who tread their chosen paths to completion will likely meet at the apex of compassion, love, and humility, even if their starting points are different.

Research Your Role Models

If you have role models, research their lives. Read memoirs and autobiographies if available, browse through their Wikipedia pages and watch videos, weigh both the positive aspects of their lives and the critiques leveled against them. Getting to know the ins and outs of people's lives is important. It gives a nuanced view that is rooted in authentic human complexity. Interestingly enough, the imperfections we find —so long as they are not disqualifying atrocities (remember to assign good intent and try to see things from the prevailing perspective of each period)—can actually help us move forward and take action. The reasoning is simple: "If such and such did this and that despite his or her imperfections, then I can do it as well."

Expand Your Circle of Care

Take good care of yourself, your family, and your friends. If you have a surplus of time, energy, and money, consider expanding your circle of care. There is good evidence to show that caring for others can lead to moral development, just as moral development can lead to caring.

Practice Moderating Behaviors

You may already have begun appraising your beliefs and values in relation to the attraction-repulsion principle. Take it a step further by creating a written list of likes and corresponding dislikes. Once you've uncovered strong aversions (we all have one or two), then make sure to practice moderating behaviors for balance. Recall that the goal is not to water down your beliefs, but rather to keep love for one thing from turning into hate for another.

6. Do What You Can

During a workshop I attended with Mark Victor Hanson—the co-author of the *Chicken Soup for the Soul* series—several years ago, he asked people what they thought was the most important thing about his workshop. Most participants answered by listing the things they had learned. He said it was none of that. The most important thing was what would happen when they came home. It was what they did after the workshop that mattered, not how many interesting notes they had taken.

That was a powerful lesson, one I have never forgotten. An emphasis on action was already incorporated into most of my workshops, lectures, and seminars at the time, but afterward, it became my primary focus. I realized that all my programs were for planning and that performance was the next logical step.

The same is true about the material in this book. Without action, we can relegate ideas about common ground, bridge-building, peacemaking, healing, and harmony to the realm of wishful thinking.

Correspondingly, the most important question you can ask yourself right now is: "What am I going to do when I am done reading?"

Moving from inaction to action is no easy task. Despite our best efforts, doubt, fear, and hesitancy are inherent. All human beings tend to second-guess themselves and postpone action. In the 18th Century, Edmund Burke famously posited that for evil to triumph, all that was needed was for good men to do nothing.

The same can be said about our times. As acrimony gets a tighter grip on democratic society, good people can either sit on the sidelines, debilitated by anxiety and daily distractions, or they can overcome indecision and work towards finding common ground.

...With What You Have, Where You Are

No one can change the world on their own. Still, we can all do more than we are currently doing. As I said at the beginning of this book, we can do what we can, with what we have, where we are.

Wherever you are in your journey, the following checklist can help you take the next logical steps.

✔ *Identify Divides*

Begin by looking around you and list divisions that already exist, first in your family, faith community, and neighborhood, then expand your field of vision and detect chasms that exist in race relations, political behaviors, and so on. Once you have a list of identified divides, think about where you can have an impact.

✔ *List What You Have to Work With*

In this book, we have explored a variety of methods and approaches, such as breaking the cycle of extremism, choosing a new narrative of compassion, focusing on shared humanity (merely using that term can have a positive effect and help people see the elements we all share), strengthening human bonds through experiences, engaging in structured dialogue, progressing from self-care to world-care, and more. In addition to these approaches, you already have access to what you've gathered through your education and experience. Make an inventory of everything that you've learned that can be of use.

✔ *Develop Your Skills*

The development of any skill takes practice. If you are serious about finding common ground, you will make a commitment to continual improvement in you area of choice. The better you become, the more you can do.

✔ Join/Gather a Group

This kind of work is rarely done single-handedly. Look around and join groups that are already working on finding common ground or gather a group of healers on your own. There is a list of organizations at the back of this book that can help you get started.

✔ Take Action

Nothing substitutes action. For things to get done, someone needs to do something. Take the first step, then the next step... and before you know it, something has been done, and you've been a part of doing it.

Be Actively Hopeful

The term 'hope' often indicates a passive state of sitting around and waiting. I prefer being actively hopeful—purposely cultivating a sense of compassion within myself and doing my best to influence the outside world.

An ancient Hindu prayer encourages the believer to lift the veil and see God everywhere. Likewise, we, the willing, should practice the art of lifting the ideological veil and seeing shared humanity everywhere. We must be mindful of all the elements that tie us together. We breathe the same air, drink the same water, and are made of the same stardust.

We need to work towards a new social contract. One where we first affirm each other's humanity and argue civically about ideological differences without becoming enemies. An important first step can be to silently affirm "I see our shared humanity" or "we belong to the same tribe" during all human interactions—especially when we disagree with someone. It may feel unnatural at first, but with time and practice, it will become instinctive.

Let Us Work Together...

The ideas and strategies that I've provided in this book are waiting to be put to good use. Please, stay in touch and keep me informed about the impact of your efforts.

Gudjon Bergmann
Email: bergmann@gudjonbergmann.com
Website: www.gudjonbergmann.com

Appendix: Bridge-Building Perspectives

Most people are familiar with the parable of the three blind men who were attempting to describe an elephant. One held the trunk, another the tail, and the third held the belly while they argued vehemently about which one of them was right in their description of the elephant. In their own way, they were all correct. Each held a vital piece of the puzzle. Ken Wilber articulates this idea of multiple perspectives well:

"I have one major rule: Everybody is right. More specifically, everybody—including me—has some important pieces of truth, and all of those pieces need to be honored, cherished, and included in a more gracious, spacious, and compassionate embrace. To Freudians I say, Have you looked at Buddhism? To Buddhists I say, Have you studied Freud? To liberals I say, Have you thought about how important some conservative ideas are? To conservatives I say, Can you perhaps include a more liberal perspective? And so on, and so on, and so on... At no point have I ever said: Freud is wrong, Buddha is wrong, liberals are wrong, conservatives are wrong. I have only suggested that they are true

but partial. My critical writings have never attacked the central beliefs of any discipline, only the claims that the particular discipline has the only truth—and on those grounds I have often been harsh. But every approach, I honestly believe, is essentially true but partial, true but partial, true but partial. And on my own tombstone, I dearly hope that someday they will write: He was true but partial..."

True but partial is a statement that I resonate with deeply. It describes my efforts in a nutshell. That is why I sought input from a range of people in this appendix. I wanted to give you an opportunity to explore the core concepts of social harmony and bridge-building from a variety of angles, to see viewpoints and dimensions that I had not adequately covered.

One Question, Eighteen Answers

In late August and early September 2018, I sent out a questionnaire. On the following pages, you will find eighteen answers to the question: What is the best bridge-building technique you have come across or used?

I urge you to take time to get to know all the contributors and the organizations that they represent. Look at their websites and explore their work. If you like what you see, please share their work through your social media channels. All of them are making a positive difference in the world and should be celebrated.

Note: I did not read any of the answers until after I had finished writing the book. The parallels you'll see have arisen naturally and without any coordination.

* * *

What is the best bridge-building technique you have come across or used?

Yehuda Stolov
Interfaith Encounter Association
www.interfaith-encounter.org

"When we analyze the disapproving attitudes that many in our communities have for each other we realize that these are not the result of an educated decision that it is impossible to live together. On the contrary: negative attitudes result from the generalization of individual cases of negativity, which creates prejudices and off-putting stereotypes that result in a negative image of the 'other.'

The problem with such images is that they are psychologically rooted and it is not enough to explain the actual reality to counteract them. To uproot them we need an experience that will be psychologically significant. The interfaith encounter in which participants truly and deeply meet the 'other' face-to-face, provides such an experience and can be profoundly transformative.

Interfaith encounter focuses on themes that relate to the foundation of the respective cultures and touches on issues that have deep existential meaning for the participants, even for the most secular among them. Discussing together how one relates to religion and religious texts and ideas allows us to address core issues of identity and meaning and to find shared values. The discussion becomes much more intimate than just an exchange of opinions and gives room for the exposure of the humanity of the 'other,' which happens when people really look into each other's eyes. Moreover, this focus reveals large degrees of similarities between participants' traditions. This idea of discovering shared values may sound pedestrian but can be a tremendous revelation for participants. Finally, this angle allows for a constructive way to discuss differences. In this way, participants train themselves to develop friendships with people they disagree with, which is the real challenge we face.

Consequently, an interfaith encounter is not only relevant for those who enjoy interfaith dialogue or learning for their own sake. Interfaith encounters are important for any person who lives in a split society, as it gives ordinary people an avenue to make an actual contribution towards real peace—directly, without being dependent on their leaders. Knowing and understanding the 'other' directly, in turn, alleviates the fear from all members of their community and thus improves the quality of life for participants.

An interfaith encounter is a meaningful conversation in which participants exchange ideas on issues that have existential significance for them, and consequently get to know one another in a more intimate way. It reveals similarities and helps build bridges between people. At the same time, it enables people to share their differences in a constructive, respectful way, which allows the conversation to proceed and indeed deepen without defensiveness or anyone feeling threatened. In this way, interfaith encounter enables its participants to develop friendships with those they disagree with and had even been in fear of previously; this of course is the real challenge of peacebuilding in the Holy Land.

The most common way to conduct an interfaith encounter is through joint learning of our respective religions, traditions, and cultures. In the Holy Land, these carry existential meaning for everyone and can be used to connect any group of people. However, other platforms of in-depth exchange may work better for specific groups of people: music, literature, shared vocation or interest, etc.

Through the transformative power of interfaith encounter, people abandon the prejudices and stereotypes they hold of each other, replacing them with a direct and real understanding that leads to respect, trust, and friendship."

Sari Heidenreich
United Religions Initiative
www.uri.org

"This may seem simple, but the technique that I have seen work time and time again, in a variety of places around the globe, is bringing people together to serve in their community. The act of serving side-by-side with someone is an intensely bonding experience, one that helps you see that, no matter what else you might not agree on, you do agree on something—the value of this project. So, whether it be a construction project, a park clean-up, building toilets, providing disaster relief, or any number of other things, if you have a group of people that you need to bring into positive contact with one another—get them serving together!"

Rabbi Jack Moline
Interfaith Alliance
www.interfaithalliance.org

"Listening is the best technique for bridge-building. It is the behavior that best models humility (which is not thinking less of yourself but thinking of yourself less). True listening involves the ability to restate what another is saying, not manipulating what you hear to give yourself an opening to outdo another."

Marilyn Turkovich
Charter for Compassion
www.charterforcompassion.org

"I am convinced that telling our stories is the best bridge-building technique that can be used in getting individuals of different ages, races and ethnic backgrounds together. I remember many decades ago listening to a lecture by the famed psychologist Carl Rogers. He talked about the work he was doing among a group of people from Northern Ireland and the Republic of Ireland. In sharing their stories they affirmed what Plato told us, and I paraphrase here: "be open to others because they too may be suffering just as you are." There is an approach I have used for years that I learned from Roberto Chene, a proponent of re-evaluation counseling. In a fifteen minute period you can invite two people, who don't necessarily know one another to come together and observe a few rules: listen unconditionally to the other, don't ask questions, respect each other's privacy and keep what you have heard to yourselves. Allow the first person to speak for 5 minutes telling the highlights of their life story—revealing what have been the milestones in his/her life and the other person just listening—no questions, no gestures, just pure presence gifted to the speaker. Switch roles. Same rules. Finally, allow for shared talking. Most often, without retelling stories, the collective analysis reveals the similarities of our life experiences. There are other questions to pursue in the use of re-evaluation counseling and each brings in more depth, understanding, and acceptance of the other, and even acknowledges and appreciates the "other" who may eventually become a part of "one's own" family."

Rev. Dirk Ficca
Twin Cities Social Cohesion Initiative
www.tcsci.org

"In general, it's all about relationships and their humanizing character. So the short answer is: Get as many people and communities face-to-face with each other as possible—preferably across divides—for positive encounters and constructive conversations. To flesh that out a bit, I can further suggest the following: Begin by understanding and respecting people for who they are – their experience, perspective, needs, aspirations, and motivations, reach out to those still making up their minds about 'who's in' and 'who's out,' do everything through partnership, provide safe environments and inclusive processes for those impacted to share their concerns and aspirations, and to have a decisive role in decision-making, and infuse the public discourse with positive images and constructive rhetoric."

Beth A. Broadway
InterFaith Works of Central New York
www.interfaithworkscny.org

"InterFaith Works views "dialogue" as an inclusive, strategic process; hence, dialogue is a facilitated, multisession discussion that has the potential to build trust, respect, and understanding among diverse groups of people. The ability to come together and find common ground on which to stand and a means to move forward on critical social issues even when there is disagreement is part and parcel of dialogue. A "dialogue circle" refers to the group of people that participate in a dialogue over 4-6 sessions of 2 hours per session. Dialogue circle meetings are facilitated by two trained co-facilitators who have different identities from one another (i.e., ideally they will represent different genders and ethnicities) and are reflective of the group's participants. Dialogue facilitators have experience in both the topic under discussion and with group leadership.

Facilitators use discussion guides that are designed to build relationships among the group and to discuss specific areas of concern, such as racism, interfaith relations, workplace tensions or other forms of stereotyping. The content of these guides serve as meeting agendas and reading sources to focus the dialogue. An initial step in the dialogue process is that participants develop ground rules for how they will talk with one another in the group setting. Specific exercises are used to encourage and elicit discussion. One such exercise allows participants to get to know one another personally, discuss perspectives and solutions relative to topical areas. The end goal remains identification of strategies for commitments to personal and community actions.

A key assumption about dialogue circles is that participants should be ready to listen and learn from others in the group. Other assumptions typically include; to identify and to understand the impact of stereotypes, bias, and racism in our culture at both personal and structural levels; to develop the understanding and skills necessary for sustained dialogue regarding sensitive issues; to cultivate new relationships and friendships; to envision a future that provides justice and opportunity for all on many levels: personal, social, educational, economic and political; and to recognize that community members often do not have an opportunity for honest and open discussion about difficult topics in a safe space."

Dr. Güner Arslan
Dialogue Institute Austin
www.dialogueatx.org

"The best technique by far is direct interaction between individuals and groups. This might not be the easiest or the most scalable solution, but it is, based on my experience, the most effective one. I can read about others in volumes of books, I can watch documentaries or movies, I can take courses and seminars and all these would help to understand others better, but none of these is the same as looking into the eyes of a person and listening to what they have to say.

Once a "we against them" mentality takes root in a person it is very hard to uproot it by using intellectual arguments. Information can be replaced by more accurate information but emotions cannot be replaced by any information. Emotions need to be replaced with other emotions. I don't know what magic goes on inside people's hearts and minds, but I can say from experience that breathing the same air and looking into the eyes of the other does change people generally for the better. This is why at the Dialogue Institute our motto is to find excuses to bring people together."

Nora Bond
Convergence on Campus
www.convergenceoncampus.org

"Metaphorical bridge-building is perhaps even more complicated than literal bridge-building. Although best practices often rightfully focus on dialogue, active listening, and repeatedly achieving mutual understanding, the most effective practice invisibly undergirds these. Self-awareness is the primary—as in both first and essential—technique needed. If one is in dialogue, attempting to fully listen, and willing to take on another's perspective, she must first be versed in what she brought with her, what she is likely to react to, and her own processes of meaning-making.

To borrow a phrase from the Center for Courage and Renewal's Circle of Trust® Touchstones, the process requires one to "Turn to wonder." Inevitably in bridge-building there are disagreements. Instead of immediately reacting, assuming one's superiority, or judging, the phrase calls us deeper into what, in ourselves, is responding. Our values, identities, and histories are ever-present, filtering our perceptions and ready to be summoned at first notice. If one is attempting to bridge-build with a person of a different faith but has a deeply rooted perception of the other faith as dangerous, there will be only negligible progress. If one is attempting to bridge-build with someone who reminds her of a childhood bully, there will also be only negligible progress. What a bridge-builder brings to the engagement is not inconsequential. Thus, when one feels that impulse—"I must be wary of anyone who practices this faith, I am inclined to not like you because you remind me of him"—she must recognize it and turn to wonder. What is it being provoked in me? How will I respond to myself, before I proceed? Am I in a place to host this conversation, knowing what it will bring up for me? How should I proceed, if my goal is really to co-create? Of all the best practices for bridge-building, self-awareness is the foundation. Only by welcoming and examining our impulses (which come from the least informed but most defensive parts of our brain) can we be open to bridge-building authentically and sustainably."

Rev. Jon Mundy
All Faiths Seminary International
www.allfaithsseminary.org

"Obviously, the best bridge-building technique comes in the acceptance of responsibility for my own thoughts and actions, which comes in the deep realization of the most fundamental law there is in the Universe, again to quote the Course:

If I intervened between your thoughts and their results, I would be tampering with a basic law of cause and effect; the most fundamental law there is. I would hardly help you if I depreciated the power of your own thinking. This would be in direct opposition to the purpose of this course. It is much more helpful to remind you that you do not guard your thoughts carefully enough. You may feel that at this point it would take a miracle to enable you to do this, which is perfectly true. You are not used to miracle-minded thinking, but you can be trained to think that way. All miracle workers need that kind of training.
T-2.VII.1:4-10

Everything is up to me. It's how I choose to see my brother that matters. I love the definition of Jesus from the Course.

Jesus was a man but saw the face of Christ in all his brothers and remembered God.
C-5.II.1

i.e., Jesus saw the false without accepting it as true."

Dr. Mehnaz M. Afridi

The Holocaust, Genocide and Interfaith Education Center at Manhattan College

www.hgimanhattan.com

"I use various tools to build bridges and one the most effective one is how you tell a story when there are conflicting narratives in a room. I work with many Catholics, Muslims, and Jews to build bridges and have been able to deal with very challenging topics by following some hard but simple rules: Listen to the narrative of the other, emotional responses are not effective, acknowledge the pain of the other, be self-critical, and be truthful about the scars of your community in the past.

For example, I take from the following lessons:

In 2016, I visited Berlin, Germany where I was invited for the release of the third German edition of responses to Die Sonnenblume by Simon Wiesenthal as I was invited to write a response from a Muslim perspective. I met many Germans who were interested in my role as a Muslim woman teaching Islam and also directing a Holocaust Center. Their questions came from shock and dismay perhaps a backlash, I wondered as they inquired how I could possibly be entrapped in two polarizing and extreme visions of the world: Jewish & Muslim. The most startling comments were how I could call myself a Muslim since I did not wear the hijab and why I would be deeply committed to Holocaust education, and lastly, could I not find something better to do! Some comments horrified my American and now Berliner host such as; "Voting for Hitler was the only thing we could have done!" Awkward silence and brisk acknowledgments by the local Berliners became a stark message to me that somehow my identity was sterilized and my work on the Holocaust had been battered in the most apologetic country of European crimes during World War II. I continued to speak with the local Germans and ask questions that they had never confronted, not about the Holocaust but their own feelings of loss as they experienced a million Syrians migrate into what they assumed was only a German country. These locals became engaged in these issues by building an understanding between them and myself.

Recently, I was invited to Miami, Florida to speak for the local Muslim community on Jewish-Muslim relations, then I was invited to speak to a few leaders. I sat with five respectful and professional Muslim men who are considered leaders in the Muslim-American communities in Miami, a city with a large Jewish population. I was there to have a conversation about Muslim perceptions of Jews and how we can change our view taking into consideration the principles of Islam. I was asked the following questions about Jews: "Don't you think they control political events? Aren't they all rich?" Some of them had never asked those questions openly and I was there as a Muslim to respond. This intimate conversation is one of several I have had about the perception of Jews in Muslim communities, whether they are Turkish, Indian, Pakistani, Saudi, Iraqi, or others. We discussed the Shoah, and I was instantly confronted with questions about other genocides in comparison. This discussion was immensely important in many ways: first, it allowed male Muslim leaders to listen to a Muslim woman speak about Jews; second, it offered a reference point in the religion when they go out in the community; and finally, they were open to pursuing the deepening of Jewish–Muslim relations. One of the many issues that were brought up was the concern about the Qur'anic scriptures that discuss Jews or Christians in a negative light. The Qur'an has many such verses that can be negative and ambiguous for the non-Muslim and especially Muslims. And, on the other hand, my work with Jewish community leaders is led by the following question at times: "Is the Qur'an anti-Semitic?" My response is clearly: no. Such a response requires that we understand the Qur'an and the representations of Jews in the Islamic tradition. Teaching at a Lasallian Catholic College as a Muslim woman both Islam and the Holocaust has been an amazing opportunity and I can confidently say that my work at the Center and the dept. of Religious Studies is in itself a living testimony of interfaith work.

These incidences and many more have strengthened my work on the Shoah and my Islamic identity and both Muslims and Jews compelled me to think about memory. The challenges I face are Holocaust denial, relativization or blatant anti-Semitism seeped in the words: Israel and Zionism. The challenges I face personally as a Muslim is the Islamophobia on the streets, the perceptions of Muslims, women and immigrant policies that have isolated many. Most of these challenges have been wrought with how we through generations in these specific communities think of one another or as I say "remember each other" or even "acknowledge" one another's history? My work on the Holocaust, Shoah is about bringing the stories of millions alive because I believe that as people of different identities and communities, we need to speak up for one another. How I ask, can we build bridges in this climate?

How has one learned to recall the "other's" tradition? What moments in history are the ones that define us and those that do not? David Rieff's book In Praise of Forgetting: Historical Memory and its Ironies, he asks the important questions of memory, tradition, and ethics. He further questions how and what we choose to commemorate, forgive and forget. What shall I Never forget; the loss, the death and the need for humans to kill and destroy my identity? David Rieff's chapter entitled, "Must we deform the past in order to preserve it," resonated with me in two ways; one that memory of a particular past is framed morally by human beings as either positive or negative in this case a deformed memory as Rieff puts it, two that Nostalgia (or how one recollects the past) can protect or destroy memory as he further states: "At some point in time, will not Nazi atrocities, collaboration, even the Shoah itself become …plain history?" My question is how do we transition our own memories that are not only the creation of our community's memory but how do we deform the memories of the other to protect our own narrative? I wondered many times, whether I ever did crawl out of my zone and confront the memory of someone else's' past? And does this move have a morality in order for us to move beyond the memory of an old enemy, perpetrator, and murderer? This was what compelled some of the work I did in my book but more importantly, I wanted to ask some deeper questions about the construction of who we are against someone else's sensation of memory."

Rev. Scott Quinn
Marin Interfaith Council
www.marinifc.org
www.scottquinn.net

"The best bridge-building technique is active listening with an open heart and mind. When we meet someone who is "different" or "other," can we suspend our pre-conceived notions long enough to see a whole human being rather than a label or belief system? For instance, if you are a cis-gender Christian and have a deep conversation with a person who is Muslim or Transgender, you are not meeting with Islam or the entire Transgender community, you are meeting with a full human being for whom their religion or gender-identity is a key part of their human experience, but it neither defines nor determines their entire person-hood. We meet individuals not religious or ethnicities or sexual orientations or any other label/group. When doing active listening, we also listen not just for a person's beliefs and views, but we are also curious about experiences that form those perspectives. We say, "That's a fascinating perspective that is different than mine. Would you be willing to share with me an experience you've had that shapes your view?" We are always encountering a unique human being, whose experiences, gifts, and paradoxes exceed any single affiliation or label."

Rev. Rhonda Schienle
World AWAKE
www.worldawakeinc.org

"To listen often with care and compassion for and with others is one of the best bridge-building techniques I have utilized. Listening and acknowledging another human being is a wonderful gift to give and fosters bridge-building. Also, when one remembers what another believes, does not take away or remove anything from who you are."

Clay Boykin
Men's Fellowship Network
www.clayboykin.com

"My father traveled and lived around the world as an agriculture economist. His role was to help increase crop and livestock yields. Rather than going in with a preconceived idea of who the people were and what needed to be done, Dad took time beforehand to study the history of the culture and region seeking to understand the background as to why farming and ranching was being done the way it was. This provided a frame of reference that enabled him to engage meaningfully with his clients whether they were in Africa, Syria, Pakistan or Iran. He would tell me, first seek to understand and then be understood."

Rev. Laura M. George
The Oracle Institute
www.theoracleinstitute.org

"What Maslow's Hierarchy of Needs, the Spectrum of Consciousness, and Integral Theory plainly reveal is that human evolution is not moving as quickly as we would want, nor as quickly as the challenges of the 21st Century demand. In the Post-Modern Age, we are witnessing a clash of cultures the world has never seen. Why? Because the Spectrum of Consciousness is so varied that there are barbarians (i.e., people with impulsive, low-level needs and drives) walking the earth alongside avatars (i.e., people who have reached or are closing in on the advanced state of enlightenment). While this may sound hyperbolic, it is the truth. Incidentally, objective truth does exist, despite the current trend toward dismantling and debasing it.

To clarify my point, let me briefly summarize some of the conclusions we have reached at The Oracle Institute, thanks to our careful study of Integral Theory: When humans existed thousands of years ago, everyone operated at just a few levels of existence. You were either in the aristocratic and privileged class and you exploited your power, you were a merchant or a warrior and you enjoyed a modicum of control over your life experience, or you were a serf who had nothing more to hope for than ample food, shelter, and sex.

But today, we see many classes or levels of the human experience. There still are people struggling for their very existence, but at the other end of the spectrum are those who have not only managed to overcome all base level needs—including materialism—they have begun to self-actualize and reach states of non-duality! Such humans did not exist in the past, except as leaders of religious movements (e.g.: Jesus, Buddha). So to even speak of "social harmony" means that there now are enough humans on the planet who hold this value as a treasured goal.

To bridge the ever-widening gap between the spiritual "haves" and the material "have-nots" (which is an extreme oversimplification of the spectrum) requires a great deal of expertise. At Oracle, we call this divide the "God Gap," and we rack our brains and search our hearts every day to figure out how to bridge the great chasm created by the resultant culture wars. Would that there existed a magic key—just one key that could unlock the evolutionary impulse in everyone! The reality is that there is no one magic key. Instead, there are numerous approaches to spreading social harmony and those methods differ depending toward whom you wish to apply the balm of love. For every meme loves. The issue is to what extent humans are capable of extending their love, whether it be a tribal extension, an ethnocentric sharing, or a global comprehension of interconnectedness that leads to the purest form of social harmony.

Consequently, those of us who wish to spread altruistic morals need to have a firm grasp of how humans "transcend and include" their worldviews. Everyone has the capacity for growth, and collectively we slowly are reaching greater levels of social harmony. Yet individually we contribute to the expansion of altruism and enlightened values—such as social harmony—only after we experience the satiation of lower level needs (e.g., transcending poverty). Even then, only some of us will reach the higher states of consciousness, which allow us to feel empathy toward our fellow man, interfaith acceptance, and social egalitarianism.

To summarize, spreading social harmony is possible only when an individual and his culture are properly evaluated and then realistically addressed. Like a doctor making a diagnosis and giving a prescription, peacebuilders need the skillset to evaluate a person's capacity to live harmoniously and then suggest the correct approach to raise spiritual standards. There is no quick fix, just the potential for achieving incremental, lasting, positive change."

Steve Harper
The Ripple Effect
www.ripplecentral.com

"In my work and research, I have found that every human being has some very basic but important requirements that have to be met before he or she can be fully engaged with other people. All humans have an innate need to feel seen, heard and understood on the most basic level. When these initial conditions are met then people allow themselves to feel or to be seen as useful, important, appreciated and even loved.
Though it seems like it might take a long time to help make conditions perfect for someone to feel all of that, it really doesn't. It just takes a mindful approach to an engagement with someone to accelerate the connection and relationship building process.

The best technique to build the essential bridge of connection is to be inquisitive about them. Asking what I call origin-focused questions can give tremendous insight into their background and backstory. One of my favorite questions is "Where are you from originally?" Everyone comes from somewhere and there's often a really enlightening story about how they got from where they were to where they are right now. It's a softball question that people unconsciously appreciate because it allows them to answer with the context and content they are absolutely experts in—their life. I find that this simple question immediately relaxes people and if you're prepared to spur the conversation on with some inquisitive follow-up questions, your rapport grows stronger. Their story provides you with a pretty incredible and insightful look into who this person is at their core."

Dr. Elizabeth Debold
One World in Dialogue
www.oneworldindialogue.com
www.elizabethdebold.com

"I don't know that bridge-building can ever actually be a "technique." The word "technique" implies something instrumental. "I" over here, act on "you" over there, for a specific purpose through which you become an instrument to achieve my goal, aim, or desire. To build a bridge to another person with views or opinions that are very different from my own, I cannot approach through the comfortable distance of applying a technique. To build a bridge, I must be the bridge—through my attentive listening, interest, and not knowing. I start from knowing that we share a common humanity, no matter what. We become who we are, with the beliefs that we have, through very understandable reactions and responses to the opportunities and difficulties in our lives.

Listening, interest, and not knowing are not a technique. They cannot be faked or manufactured for the moment. In a highly charged situation, such pretense will be seen through very quickly. Listening means to listen with the aim of understanding what another is saying without an agenda of one's own. How can we understand another human being in their terms, not ours? To do so, one listens not from the analytical, judging mind, but from the whole of our experience. Mind, body, and heart attuned to the other human being, seeking resonance and wondering at what seems dissonant. For this, one brings interest—a genuine curiosity that is not seeking for itself. Being truly interested is an act of compassion. And to keep our interest alive and open, we need to come from an inner position of not already knowing. We don't prejudge or nod along with what someone is saying, because we want to take their words in fresh, new, and encounter them, coming from this unique person, on their own. It calls us to ask genuine questions, not to interrogate another or to assume that we understand. And it calls us to be sensitive to the space between us, the field of intimacy that arises through such deep attention to another human being. Such intimacy can be intimidating or too much, which we need to be aware of also, so that we allow another human to have the space and dignity to be themselves."

Linda Marks
MIFA (Metropolitan Inter-Faith Association)
www.mifa.org

"In my experience, bridge-building is most effective and most sustainable when it happens gradually and in small steps. It is not shocking or unusual for us to have natural preferences for what we are accustomed to. Change, and embracing differences, requires us to stretch ourselves beyond what is comfortable, and it takes energy.

We can try to use our will to remove biases, but when we do this, we are dealing with abstractions, as when we say, "I must learn to be more comfortable with a person of a different race, faith, or sexual orientation." We're likely to fail with this approach. But taking small steps to be with and present to someone quite different leads to sustainable growth and openness. Simply sharing a brief conversation with a person we normally wouldn't encounter can start the process. The more we do it, the more we learn to be comfortable and confident in taking the next steps."

Rev. Stephen Kinney
The Front Porch Project
www.frontporchaustin.org

"I have found that bringing people together through music or art (perhaps this functions as that "third thing"?) provides a way to transcend the usual oppositions to community. That is, by directing our attention to something beautiful outside of ourselves enables us to forget ourselves long enough to let "the other" in. Overcoming self-consciousness opens us to broader/ deeper horizons. "Ground Rules" are helpful here: I extend the invitation to recognize that when we welcome the other (hospitality), we may discover that our differences may be enriching rather than threatening.

We use the metaphor of "The Front Porch" to invite people to gather together in non-instrumental ways to pay attention and become aware of the gifts around and between us. It's an attitude for opening the heart to the other (a.k.a., humility) that promotes suspending our own limited perspectives long enough to be penetrated by the presence and ideas of others. Social interpenetration, as such, leads to learning new things and to co-creating and partnering with others. It's a way of expanding our horizons."

Resources

The following list of resources can aid in your work towards finding common ground. It includes a list of organizations, TED talks, YouTube videos, and books.

Organizations

- NAIN (North American Interfaith Network)
  www.nain.org
- Parliament of the World's Religions
  www.parliamentofreligions.org
- URI (United Religions Initiative)
  www.uri.org
- Charter for Compassion
  www.charterforcompassion.org
- Convergence on Campus
  www.convergenceoncampus.org
- Interfaith Youth Core
  www.ifyc.org
- Dialogue that Depolarizes
  www.buildingpeacebypeace.org

- Dignity Dialogues
  www.dignitydialogues.com
- Compassion Course
  www.compassioncourse.org
- Compassion Summit
  www.compassionsummit.org
- MIFA (Metropolitan Inter-Faith Association)
  www.mifa.org
- Religions for Peace
  www.religionsforpeace.org
- Dialogue Institute Austin
  www.thedialoginstitute.org/austin/
- Men's Fellowship Network
  www.mensfellowship.net
- Tanenbaum
  www.tanenbaum.org
- One World in Dialogue
  www.oneworldindialogue.com
- Goldin Institute
  www.goldininstitute.org
- Compassionate Listening
  www.compassionatelistening.org
- iACT (Interfaith Action of Central Texas)
  www.interfaithtexas.org
- Interfaith Alliance
  www.interfaithalliance.org
- Alliance for Peacebuilding
  www.allianceforpeacebuilding.org
- National Coalition for Dialogue and Deliberation
  www.ncdd.org

- Center for Interfaith Relations
  www.centerforinterfaithrelations.org
- Interfaith Encounter Association
  www.interfaith-encounter.org
- The Elijah Interfaith Institute
  www.elijah-interfaith.org
- The Interfaith Observer (media)
  www.theinterfaithobserver.org
- The Pluralism Project
  www.pluralism.org
- Kaufman Interfaith Institute
  www.gvsu.edu/interfaith
- More in Common
  www.moreincommon.com
- Scarboro Missions
  www.scarboromissions.ca
- Interfaith Amigos
  www.interfaithamigos.com

TED talks
www.ted.com

- Megan Phelps-Roper: I grew up in the Westboro Baptist Church. Here's why I left.
- Karen Armstrong: My wish: The Charter for Compassion
- Jonathan Haidt: The moral roots of liberals and conservatives
- Amy Edmondson: How to turn a group of strangers into a team

- Azim Khamisa and Ples Felix: What comes after tragedy? Forgiveness
- Nabila Alibhai: Why people of different faiths are painting their houses of worship yellow
- Chelsea Shields: How I'm working for change inside my church
- Rabbi Lord Jonathan Sacks: How we can face the future without fear, together
- Erez Yoeli: How to motivate people to do good for others

YouTube Videos
www.youtube.com

- The Interfaith Amigos: Breaking the taboos of interfaith dialogue
  https://youtu.be/tPnZArtsG_c
- Betty Williams: Shameless Idealists
  https://youtu.be/OIJFNpPqj-w
- Padraig O'Malley: The Peacemaker Q&A
  https://youtu.be/9CKsEw25B8g
- Yehuda Stolov: 12 Faces of Hope
  https://youtu.be/qJXoLgN9L4k
- Dirk Ficca: Interview
  https://youtu.be/vg9_g_fbwl4
- Mehnaz Afridi: Interview
  https://youtu.be/vMFd28zIj_4
- Daniel Kahneman: Thinking Fast vs. Thinking Slow
  https://youtu.be/PirFrDVRBo4

- Eboo Patel: To narrow toxic divides, students build bridges between faiths
  https://youtu.be/7JGNPX3b5LQ

Books

- *The Righteous Mind* – Jonathan Haidt
- *Thinking, Fast and Slow* – Daniel Kahneman
- *Twelve Steps to a Compassionate Life* – Karen Armstrong
- *How Can I Help* – Paul Gorman and Ram Dass
- *Non-Violent Resistance (Satyagraha)* – Mohandas K. Gandhi
- *Long Walk to Freedom* – Nelson Mandela
- *Out of Many Faiths* – Eboo Patel
- *Thank you for Arguing* – Jay Heinrichs
- *Changing Minds* – Howard Gardner
- *Influence* – Robert Cialdini
- *Rising Out of Hatred* – Eli Saslow
- *Religious Literacy* – Stephen Prothero
- *Strength to Love* – Martin Luther King. Jr.

About the Author

Born in Iceland in 1972, Gudjon Bergmann moved to the USA in 2010 and became a U.S. citizen in 2013. He is an ordained Interfaith Minister, experienced speaker, a devoted husband, amateur musician, and proud father of two.

Bergmann has written over twenty-five books, both works of fiction and nonfiction. His two novels are spiritual, but not mindlessly positive, mysterious, but don't revolve around criminal elements, and philosophical, but not so deep as to put the reader to sleep. His nonfiction books are practical and to the point. He has written extensively about self-development and spirituality, including books on yoga, meditation, smoking cessation, stress management, interfaith and more.

For more visit www.gudjonbergmann.com

Made in the USA
Coppell, TX
21 July 2022